Male Body Language that Attracts Women

Male Body Language that Attracts Women

by

Tony Wood

*How to turn women on
in business and in personal life
without saying a word*

1stbooks - rev.01/21/00

About the Book

Turn women on...without saying a word.

Why do some men have all the luck with women? They get the promotions at work from their women bosses. They close more sales to women buyers. They get more dates. And, you know they get more sex.

What are they doing that you are not?

In today's world, it is important for men to have very positive relationships with women. That's why <u>Male Body Language That Attracts Women</u> was written. This book can help men become aware of how approaching women, talking with them, looking at them, and sitting and standing in different positions have a strong impact on their relationships. Body language can be a potent tool for men to attract and persuade women to get what they want. *This book shows you how.*

Unfortunately, many men know nothing about body language. They are turning women off without even knowing they are doing so. By learning about the secrets of male body language, men will gain insight into how they can neutralize the negative non-verbal messages that turn women off, as well as *learn how to send positive body language messages that attract women, encourage attention, and heighten sexual interest and arousal.* This provocative book can help men achieve whatever they desire from women without saying a word.

Table of Contents

Author's Preface

As a student and practitioner of mass communications techniques, I became aware early in my life that body language could provide a forceful and effective way to send messages to others. Most people never think about the body language.

Subtle looks, expressions and poses communicate to each of us every day. We "read" these expressions on others' faces and they help us to understand messages being sent to us, including telling us what others feel and think.

As an example, you see a woman sobbing, holding her baby, rocking back and forth and you know something is wrong. You see a policeman holding up his hand, and you know he wants traffic to stop. If you are waiting in a checkout line and a clerk signals you with her hand, you might step forward or move to another counter. These are all body language signals are forms of communications.

After you think about it a little while, you realize that you read the body language of others all the time, and you use body language yourself consciously or unconsciously to send messages to others. For instance, how many times today did you nod your head in agreement? You probably wave often to friends at work or in your neighborhood.

When a loved one dies, you may hug a family member a little more firmly and hold them a minute longer than usual. You want to convey a special bond or share an intense feeling in a moment of grief, compassion and sorrow.

In a heated moment, you may stop someone from speaking by holding up your hand, palm forward, jutting it before *their* mouth. If you are very angry, you might ball your fist, show more of your teeth, open your eyes wider and flare your nostrils.

An older man who lives on my street has two ways that he waves to say hello. In one case, he simply raises his hand and shakes it from side to side a little, just as most people do. But if he really likes a person, he closes the last three fingers on his hand, points his index finger and thumb high toward the sky and shakes his wrist vigorously. He changes his body language to convey a more intense appreciation of the friendship that he wants to express.

All these uses of body language convey unmistakable messages to the various people to whom they are intended to communicate. Most people have experienced the differences between a simple hug that says "hello" when you stop by a relative's house, and the hug that says "we'll all miss you" when you are about to leave on an extended trip away from home.

At first, when you begin to study body language, you may not realize that the difference signals are subtle and happen quickly. They can be hard to notice. Yet, you know they occur. Perhaps the lack of conscious attention to body language has a lot to do with the training we received in oral language skills while in school. Our conscious mind may be concentrating so hard on listening to and decoding words, then translating them into concepts, that the most obvious level of visual body language communication gets little or no attention.

Are men and women different when it comes to using body language? I believe they are. Men do not plan their body language. They do what comes naturally. This is the big difference between men and women. Very few men are aware of their body language or consciously use body language.

Women, on the other hand, study their own body language and the body language of other women. Throughout their life time, women develop and practice body language. It starts in their early years and gains intensive scrutiny in their teenage years, continuing on through womanhood. Women adopt many poses and movements. They use body language to enhance their relationships.

While men respond to female body language, they appear completely unaware of what women are doing intentionally, unless the female body language is exaggerated. Women who become very adept at body language increase their chances of getting what they want from men. For centuries, body language has been one of the primary forms of persuasion that women have used to influence men. Women continue to have an edge in interpersonal communication because they have virtually mastered body language.

What you should ask yourself is, "Why don't men do the same thing?"

In earnest, this book asks why shouldn't men begin to pay greater attention to body language? Why shouldn't men use body language to get more of what they want?

I promise you that if you do begin a study of body language, you will find that there is much more it can do for you to enhance all your relationships with women.

Men can use body language to influence women in business. Men can increase the likelihood that a particular woman supervisor will like them and want to get to know them better. Men can use body language to improve their working relationship with female managers and coworkers. Men can use body language to gain a social advantage, so that women are more likely to want to talk to them and enjoy their company. And, of course, men can use body language to arouse women sexually.

Believe now that men can harness an incredible communication power when they understand male body language.

You can strongly influence women just by knowing the right ways to stand and sit that are very attractive to women. You can communicate messages that you would like to say in words, but would never dare. You can stimulate and arouse women, without them even knowing you are causing them to feel excited. In doing so, you gain an advantage. The intentional use of body language puts you in control because you can cause the reactions in women that you desire most.

How did my awareness of body language begin?

When I attended the college, I was fortunate to participate in a controlled study that involved body language. Under the direction of a speech department professor, a group of students were studied to determine the degree of attitudinal change that could be caused by asking a person to make a very mild affirmation concerning an issue they had previously expressed a negative or neutral feeling toward. For one study group, a touch or a handshake was added to measure the effect. The results amazed me. I learned through this experiment that often the slightest touch and a mild affirmation could cause a person to feel and act in a more positive way toward a position with which they had previously either stated a negative or neutral view during the pretest.

I have put this knowledge to use many times during the past twenty-five years since graduation. It has helped me build business relationships and create good first impressions over many years.

So you have a clear idea of my background, I am an advertising executive. I often have to present ideas and programs to corporate executives. I must convince them to take action and give them confidence that they are spending their money in an appropriate way. For many years I have worked for some of the largest corporations in the world. I have earned both a handsome income and many advertising awards.

Although I am not a sociologist or psychologist, my job requires me to study human behavior extensively. Please understand this: to create response, you must understand behavior. Advertising is a behavioral science. Stimuli are created (ads), placed before the subject (consumer), and a response is created (purchase decision). The advertising industry bears the fruit of Pavlov's experiments with animals.

Although my professional specialty entails communicating through printed words and images to cause people to respond in predictable ways, I have always wondered about the extent and power of body language. Since that first college experiment twenty-five years ago, I have continued to study body language and its effect on others.

My knowledge of body language has helped me to work more effectively as a consultant to corporations. In the course of daily business activities, I am constantly "reading" the body language of those in conference rooms or in private meetings.

I can recognize when my clients have doubts and concerns

by the looks on their faces or they way they fidget in their chairs. Any sales professional worth his or her salt can do the same thing.

In the past (but before I discovered the secrets to Male Body Language That Attracts Women), I had successfully encoded body language to help make a point during a presentation, or to reassure clients that they could trust in my judgment.

In certain situations, I would lay a hand on a shoulder, or gently grip an elbow at the right moment to express reassurance. The simple act of touching -- in a totally non-sexual way -- can help create friendship. These kinds of touches and poses have enhanced my success.

As I have always been aware of this unique power of physical communication, I have felt more confident in business. I knew I could "connect" with business people on an intangible level. This has helped me "win" accounts and persuade prospects to work with me. Nothing is more powerful testimony than that these techniques have worked for twenty-five years to help make me successful in a highly competitive field.

Now success in business is coming even more easily for me because I have discovered the secrets of male body language. I now know how to stimulate immediate positive relationships with women. I feel confident from the moment I meet a woman that she will feel predisposed positively toward me.

This knowledge has created a breakthrough in my own life and in my career. It is nothing less than a major personal discovery that is enhancing all my interpersonal relationships with women.

I will provide many examples in this book of situations in which female strangers have come to my assistance, paid special attention to me, or extended a personal courtesy to me within a few minutes of me being in their presence. This is a new experience for me. It feels good.

It was not always this way in dealing with women. In certain social situations, I failed miserably with women. At times, the same may have you happened to you. If you are confident meeting men, but not women, this book holds a special message for you.

I'm sure many men have experienced situations in which women have taken an instant dislike to them. Perhaps you have, too.

Why?

I always felt puzzled after such an encounter. What had I done wrong? In some cases, I didn't even get a chance to say a few words.

I have reasoned over the years that I must be doing something wrong in the body language department that affects women negatively. *But what is it?* This is a maddening question because you seldom get a second chance to ask the woman involved what caused her negative reaction.

From what I have said so far, I am sure you could see that I would be willing to change my body language if it would improve my success when communicating to women. But without a clue to my error, I could not figure out what I should do differently.

Then something happened, almost by accident.

I began to find the answers I have been seeking for years. The first clue came to me after a successful business meeting with a woman manager. She was a very difficult person to deal with, and I was warned about her highly critical nature before my first meeting with her.

The first meeting went better than expected. I was trying harder than usual to accommodate to her. I sat differently. I stood differently. I wanted her to know I was listening to her and responding to her needs.

After my second meeting with her, she began to seek my advice. She flattered me and my knowledge of her marketing problem. She was more anxious to hear my solutions. She was absolutely pleasant, smiled a great deal, and mixed in light conversation about home and family. At one point, she had to answer a telephone at a desk away from where we were seated. I felt that the way she bent to answer the phone was provocative, and caused me to notice her figure from an unusual perspective. She held that pose for several minutes while talking on the telephone, even though she could have walked around the desk to face me and continue talking.

I remember going home that evening wondering about her behavior. What had I done to cause her to be so open, friendly and even provocative toward me? I sat for several hours thinking about it. I was like a scientist studying the results of an experiment. After hours of thinking, I isolated several specific poses and movements I had made in the presence of this woman over the course of our meetings. I practiced each one of these movements, adjusting feet, legs, arms, head and chest. I decided to use these same body language techniques with other women. These planned movements have become the basis of a behavior model which men can follow as a starting point.

After several weeks and many successes, I began to share this behavior model with other men. They, too, experienced remarkable results. Women managers have become more friendly, open and accommodating. You will learn about these experiences through the course of this book.

My discoveries have changed me. Now women are predisposed to meet me within minutes after I enter a room. Today, I can tell you that I, and the other men who are using these techniques, have had many positive encounters with women. We are gaining a new advantage in business and in our personal relationships.

It no longer surprises me that a woman will suddenly approach me, reach over and touch me, or sit beaming and bubbly beside me while pouring out all kinds of personal thoughts. My initial analyses of certain body language led to further experimentation. I have wanted to prove that the results of purposeful encoding of body language toward women are reproducible. I found they are. The men with whom I have shared this knowledge report similar findings.

As I put these techniques to use, I have been amazed at the results. As I write, I am working for two of the most powerful financial organizations in the world. Women managers are in charge. They are directing, assisting and helping me be successful. *They want me to succeed.* They want me to undertake more work for them. They recommend me to other managers. They have become my guardian angles and I am thankful that my knowledge of the secrets of male body language has helped me build such important relationships.

The other men who know these secrets are also continuing to enjoy success. They are learning more about themselves and how they can use body language to affect the women they meet socially and in business. Enthusiasm has continued to grow. I continue to learn more every day.

This book is your starting point. It should help you understand more about your own body language, and evaluate how you are communicating with your body in the presence of women. Every movement you make speaks volumes.

Keep your mind open to the possibilities. When you finish this book, you will know the broad strokes of this subtle communication form.

As you gain knowledge, inject your own style to the movements and poses I present to you.

As you use these techniques, it will be easy to identify what works for you.

It may take time for you to enjoy success. Don't get discouraged if you do not notice an immediate reaction. The reaction will come, but it may take time.

Remember, men and women are different. Men often react instantly, igniting like a flash fire. Women often are more like a fuse -- they are hard to light, take a while to burn, and slowly get hot prior to the explosion. Body language lights the fuse, and fans the burning. Keep working on your body language techniques and the explosion eventually comes.

What should be your first step as you start this book?

Take an honest assessment of yourself by asking these questions:

- Do you know what are you saying to women with your current body language?
- It is possible that you are communicating exactly the opposite messages that you intend to send?

- How should you change yourself?
- What is your attitude toward yourself?
- What is your attitude toward women?
- Are you pleased with the way you look?
- How can you change your body language to be more successful with women?

Most likely, you will find that changes are in order. *Make them!* Once you learn the basics of Male Body Language That Attracts Women, you will be on your way to being more successful with all your encounters with women.

1.

What can knowledge of male body language do for you?

The best way to describe the power you enjoy from understanding male body language and its effects on women is to provide insights from incidents that have occurred in my own life.

First, let me say that I am an average male, about one hundred eighty pounds, five feet ten inches tall. I consider my looks to be average. My wife tells me I am handsome and I love her for it. I have brown hair and brown eyes. Because I'm in my mid-to-late forties, flecks of gray have found their way into my hair and my mustache. I do not believe that I am particularly attractive nor unattractive to women.

Three years ago I started exercising daily, partly because of a health problem and partly to add strength to overcome back pain. A year ago, I started working out with a weight machine. During the past twelve months, my weight increased from one hundred seventy to my present one hundred eighty. I am stronger, have more muscle tone than ever and I am certain that exercise has enhanced my appearance. I recommend weight training to everyone who reads this book. If you are not in shape, start now and become physically fit.

During the past year, I have become more aware of my body. I'm more relaxed and I don't feel as self conscious as I used to because no longer is a soft stomach hanging over my belt. I have started standing straighter and sitting differently.

Eight months into my weight training program, I started wondering if I really looked more attractive to women. Could I use this new attractiveness to my advantage in business?

I found that having a pleasing appearance is only a part of

what attracts women. More importantly, I have discovered the secrets of how body movements attract women. As you read in later chapters, I will share these secrets with you. I will also share secrets about obnoxious male body movements that repel women. Certain male body movements and poses can literally cause women to flee from you.

Keep in mind that I sell to business women every day. My field, like so many others, is highly competitive. I am finding that an increasing number of women are replacing men as buyers in my field and they are now making the purchase decisions. I am a consultant and I need to keep women customers happy. I survive only if women managers request me to come back to handle more projects for them.

You should know I have not always been successful in dealing with women in business. Like so many men, I have had my share of troubles.

My first encounter with a women boss happened my first year after college. The city editor who hired me for my first job was promoted.

The new city editor was a woman. We had a cordial, but strained relationship. At the time, I could not pinpoint why we didn't work well together.

I never felt a sense of trust from her than my previous editor had accorded me. When a major story broke, she checked my sources. She did it secretly, not letting me know she was calling to confirm the story.

It wasn't a problem for me that she wanted to confirm the story herself, but it was the way that she did it. I found out because my sources phoned me to let me know about her secret calls and questions. My sources wondered if she trusted me.

I explained that it was part of her responsibility to make sure all the reporting in the newspaper was accurate. I let it go at that, and I never let her know about the call backs I received. That lack of trust between us eventually caused me to leave the newspaper.

What was it about me that caused her to want to check my work?

I was young, twenty-two at the time, but I consistently dug out good stories that were often featured on page one.

I was spunky, hardworking and had a gritty stick-to-it attitude. Thinking back now, I'm sure that my body language was confrontational. I swaggered, appeared tough and cocky. It was part of growing up a poor kid and trying to beat the odds to get any edge in life.

I wasn't about to let anyone take anything away from me without a fight.

Her calls to check my sources were an encroachment on my honesty and accuracy -- hallmarks of a good journalist. I took that as an insult and resented it.

Can you imagine the glare on my face whenever she asked me a question? Can you visualize my arms folded across my chest, staring down at her, as I stood before her desk as I answered questions about my stories?

Yes, I wanted my body language to make our conferences uncomfortable for her.

I wanted to communicate my anger and resentment.

I wanted to intimidate her physically.

Of course, it did not work.

She was a top-notch editor who had worked on the International Herald Tribune and had covered the World War II war crimes trials. A 22-year-old kid wasn't going to alter the way she performed her job.

She ignored my body language and my attitude, continued to check my sources as she saw fit, and continued to feature my writing on the front page with my by-line.

Our association did not last long.

As luck would have it, one of my feature stories earned an award from The Associated Press. Soon after, I was offered a job by the AP. I left the newspaper and went on to become a wire service newsman.

At the time, I felt relief; I was not working for *her* any more.

A second, negative episode involving a female co-worker happened some years later. I was accused of job discrimination against her in a law suit that was filed, but was later withdrawn.

Here's what happened.

It was the late seventies and I was the copy chief and public relations director of a mid-size advertising agency.

A female account executive had just been hired and together we were assigned to present designs for a new brochure to one of the agency's accounts. In the middle of the presentation meeting, to my surprise and horror, she raised her voice to a yell and sternly reprimanded the elderly owner of a privately held company.

She did not know that the agency humored the old man with iterations month after month. Planning a new brochure was his hobby. He enjoyed seeing designs -- and he had plenty of money and time on his hands. It made him happy.

The agency had been through the process with him several times over the years, and was comfortable with it.

As usual at this latest meeting, this kindly old gentleman asked to see different design treatments. The new account executive wanted to wrap the project up, perhaps to show she could drive the project to completion.

She didn't want to accept that the layouts were being rejected, and another round of design work would be required. She wanted his approval right then and demanded that the elder company manager make a decision.

She bristled because he was unwilling to accept her direction and recommendations.

The meeting ended badly.

The old man asked us to leave; for the first time I saw him angry.

She was livid.

On the way back to the office, I offered my opinion that she had made a mistake in yelling at the elderly man. Common sense told me you don't yell at clients, particularly ones that are happy to pay extra charges.

She turned her anger at me and started yelling. It was nerve racking because she was driving seventy miles per hour in the high speed lane.

Thinking back about the situation now, I realize I had no

sensitivity toward this woman.

She felt men were ignoring her and rejecting her ideas out of hand. While I still think it was inappropriate to yell at clients, she had a right to her feelings.

Even though the old gent was pleasant during the meeting, he wasn't about to accept her recommendations. His body language let her know her recommendations did not count.

When she tried to direct his attention to what she felt was important, he paid little interest.

She felt ignored and belittled in that meeting. She was right; she was.

She lost the battle. The client called to complain. The agency president removed her from the account.

Eventually, she left the agency and filed a law suit, claiming the agency discriminated against women. I was named as one of the defendants.

When the incident was investigated, it was determined that there were no grounds for the suit and it was dropped.

Why have I told you about these experiences?

My objective is simple.

Be aware of male body language and how it communicates to women.

Women can react explosively as that account executive did. Women can ignore you, distrust you and undermine your relationships with others as that editor did to me.

These are just a few of the ways women can respond to you, your attitude and your body language which tells them so much about how you feel and what you are thinking.

Today, I have changed my approach, style and body language. These changes are having a dramatic effect in my relationships with the professional women I encounter. It took two decades for me to reach this point.

Perhaps like you, I can recall many times in my past that I was totally ignored by women -- in business and social situations.

Consider this and see if it is familiar to you.

Often I have made many new business presentations,

sometimes with agency teams, sometimes alone. The most disturbing encounters were those in which I was unable to distinguish myself, nor gain any approval or commitment from potential women clients.

This was the direct opposite of the reaction I have consistently achieved with men buyers. Honestly, the reactions were dramatically different. For the most part, men would immediately give me their approval and commitment. During presentations, they would engage me in conversation, ask for advice and talk at length, opening up about their needs. I instantly knew "we connected."

Women buyers, on the other hand, were always reserved and cool to me. They tended to sit back, ask few questions, and then politely, but promptly end the presentation.

Men would call me back and talk more about their needs. Women would not. Women would be hard to follow up. Seldom did I "win the business" when a woman was involved.

How was I offensive to these women?

What was I doing wrong?

Why were they disinterested in me?

Why had I failed to impress them?

My work has always been first rate in my field and I have won many awards. I did not know what it was, but there was something about me and my body language -- that failed miserably in the presence of some women.

I was always determined to find out what this was. Now I have, and soon you will know these secrets, too.

Let me mention here that I have been happily married for more than twenty years. But even my wife reacted negatively to me the first time I tried to get to know her.

She breezed right by me the first time I tried to speak to her at a party. Nothing worked that night.

It took three more tries on my part, plus an introduction through one of her roommates, to give me a chance at a simple conversation with her ten days later.

After we got to know each other, I asked her why she had ignored me the first time I tried to meet her.

She couldn't tell me.

She was uncomfortable at the party being near me. She wanted to be in another room, away from me.

Days later, after she had the assurance of her friends that I was a nice guy, she consented to come to an informal group dinner party at the house where I and three roommates lived.

I cooked the dinner and she had a good time.

She saw me relaxed, talking with other people, laughing and being casual.

Because I was busy and involved in hosting the party, I was naturally being myself. I was not trying to impress her.

She saw me differently than what she had observed about me at the previous party. And the rest, as they say, is history.

All this transpired more than 22 years ago. Today, I recognize the differences between my first encounters with my wife, and what my body language had conveyed.

If you have experienced situations in which you instantly turn off women -- and want to reverse this negative reaction to a positive one -- this book could change your life. I have discovered the body language tools that men can use to attract and predispose women in positive ways toward men.

Consider these tools to be your body language vocabulary to communicate to women in unspoken, unconscious ways. Not all women will respond to you if you do, but many, many women will.

What can you expect by applying the knowledge in this book?

- Women will be more friendly toward you.
- Women will trust you more quickly.
- Women will begin conversations with you.
- Women will share their feelings more openly with you.
- Women will reveal more about their personal lives to you.
- Women will offer you assistance.
- Women will smile at you more often.
- Women will give you assignments and award you contracts.

- Women will invite you into stronger relationships.

There is much more that Male Body Language That Attracts Women will do for you. Certainly, like most men you are probably interested in using male body language techniques to enhance your sex life.

Male body language techniques that are revealed on the following pages can assist you in every aspect of your relationships with women. These techniques can help you get closer to women emotionally and physically.

I am certain that once you begin to apply the techniques in this book, you will present yourself in new ways that cause women to find you more attractive. You will soon experience a newer, friendlier attitude that women will display toward you.

Once you eliminate male body language that women dislike and which causes women to reject you immediately, you will enjoy a brighter future, including greater opportunities to improve your personal success and sexual satisfaction.

2.

What is body language?

People who specialize in communications have long been aware of body language. It is the unspoken messages that are sent from one person to another by the way you sit, lean, stand, gesture and move.

Even the distance you stand from another person sends a message to them. The technical term for body language is kinesics. Kinesics refers to the way people communicate through body movements and gestures, such as a raised eyebrow, a shift in posture, a wave of the arm or hand. This is non-verbal communication, and it usually works in concert with the words you speak.

You have a wide kinesics vocabulary, even though you are probably not fully conscious of it. It consists of a startling array of nonverbal signals, such as handshakes, hand holding, cuddling, postures, head positions, arms and hand movements, eye movements, facial expressions, lip movements, eye brow wrinkle movements, and dozes of other subtle ways that you move.

As a student of communication, I learned that gestures and motions vary from one culture to another. This suggests that body language is not instinctive, but learned. These movements are learned by imitating others.

Often there is no awareness on the part of the learner that he is learning what his role model is teaching him.

Unless you become keenly aware of your own body language through a book such as this one or by traveling to foreign cultures where body language customs are different, you would probably remain unaware of this unspoken form of communication all your life.

In each culture, people learn how to sit, walk, stand, hold one's hand, scratch and so on. There is an early process of teaching body language that separates boys from girls. Your role models for body language were your parents and immediate family.

Remember how your father sat at the dinner table?

Remember how he stood when he was angry at you?

Remember your mother's expressions and touch when you were sick or needed help?

These images played a role in how you developed your own body language.

Within any small segment of body language movements, there can be many sub-movements that modify the basic communication. These sub movements are like adverbs because they modify the basic message.

For instance, if a woman smiles at you, you could take this as a positive message.

On one hand, if she were to add a wink, toss her head casually to the side, and flip her hair, you might think her smile is taking on a more provocative meaning.

On the other hand, if she smiles, then looks away and resumes her normal posture, you might think her smile was only a pleasant thank you or acknowledgment, but nothing more.

As you become aware of non-verbal communication, you begin to learn how subtle it can be.

There is a famous case of a "counting horse," a vaudeville act whose trainer proclaimed that the horse could count to any number.

The trainer swore that he never signaled the animal. The horse would tap out with his hoof correctly the number someone called out from the audience.

Year after year, this animal amazed audiences, tapping correct counts with his hoof. People tried to discover the secret.

The trainer was watched closely.

The horse was watched closely.

No electronic devices were found.

The trainer stood perfectly still and made no detectable

movements.

A communications expert filmed the act and studied the film. It was discovered that the trainer blinked his eyes and wrinkled his forehead slightly each time he expected the animal to tap its hoof.

The trainer did not even know he was doing it; it was more a slight movement of expectation and hope that the animal would succeed. Once this was discovered and the trainer became aware of it, the horse could not count correctly unless he saw the trainer's full face.

This is an example of how slight body language movements can communicate to others.

Accept as fact that you are not aware of all the nonverbal messages you send to others every day.

Start your thinking about your body language at this point: virtually every move you make sends a message.

Keeping all I've had said in mind, it's time now to begin to raise your awareness of male body language. Consider the following situation, that included both nonverbal and verbal conversations, that happened at an office supply store. The events transpired within a period of about ten minutes. It involved a number of people using copiers.

The first incident: the copier breaks.

I was standing in line when one of two copy machines stopped operating. The woman customer involved, whom I will call Woman #1, was about fifty years old and wearing casual work clothes.

She read the copier's digital display. She was unsure what a blinking light indicated, so she checked the paper tray. She found it full. She reinserted the paper cassette into the machine.

The machine continued to blink.

She ignored the blinking light and pushed the start button again.

The machine did not respond. The light continued to blink.

Because I use the machine often, I looked over her shoulder and mentioned that the blinking indicated the machine required more coins.

She turned to me and said, "I had inserted thirty cents and only made one copy. It can't need any more money."

I said simply, in a pleasant voice, with my arms folded behind me, "that signal means it requires more money." I smiled and shrugged my shoulders.

Woman #1 ignored my comment and instead tried to adjust the paper cassette one more time.

When that failed again, she pressed the coin return button repeatedly. It had no effect.

She inserted another quarter.

The machine continued to blink.

She leaned over the machine toward a store counter to catch the attention of the cashier nearby.

The cashier was busy with another customer.

Woman #1 finally caught the cashier's eye and said, "This machine needs help."

The cashier returned the woman's remark with a blank stare and looked back toward the customer at her register. The cashier continued to help her current customer, never answering the plea from Woman #1.

Woman #1 pursed her lips. She squared her feet toward the cashier. Her hands fell to her hips. She stared directly at the cashier, trying to burn a hole with her eyes through the cashier.

The cashier never gave Woman #1 a second look.

Ask yourself these questions:

1) What did the body language of Woman #1 tell you?

Let's break it down.

• When I politely told Woman #1 that the paper tray wasn't the problem, but the coin box was, she ignored the advice. Remember how she tried to fix the paper cassette again? Her body language said she did not believe me.

• When she decided to ask the cashier for help, she was annoyingly aggressive. She knew the cashier was busy with another customer, but that didn't matter to her. She wanted immediate attention. She squared her feet toward the cashier, leaned forward as far as she could, stretched her neck and her right arm to get the attention of the cashier. Her frustration increased when the cashier's body language rebuffed her.

2) What did the body language of the cashier tell you?

"I'm too busy to help you" and "you don't matter" are probably two immediate thoughts that come to your mind. I've known this cashier for several years. She has often complained to me about her hours, about her workload, about how busy the store is. Customer service is one of her weakest skills, and she tells everyone how she feels with her body language.

At this point, Woman #1 was obviously frustrated. I expected her to press the issue and become obnoxious. Instead, she waited a minute, probably thinking she would try the cashier again as soon as she was free.

Fortunately, a third party was observing: the store manager.

The manager stepped in. He quickly fixed the copier, restoring it to its operating condition.

Despite his efforts, Woman #1 was not appeased. She marched out of the store.

Perhaps the message that the cashier sent to her, "you don't count to me" will stay with Woman #1 for a long time even though the manager was helpful in trying to solve the problem.

Here's what happened at the adjacent copier station while Woman #1 was having her problems:

The customer ahead of me stepped up to the copier that Woman #1 had been using.

At the second working copier was Woman #2, who played an important role in the events to follow.

Let me describe Woman #2.

Dressed in a skirt and a business jacket, she had been keeping herself busy while Woman #1 was experiencing problems.

I must admit that I never noticed if Woman #2 looked at Woman #1, or at me, during the brief exchanges I mentioned. I now know Woman #2 was fully aware of me.

Let me also add here that some of the body language techniques for men that will be revealed in his book were being used by me during these entire events. Often, as I have found many times since I began using these techniques, I am completely unaware of being observed. I have learned to trust that women will notice you -- particularly if you are making no effort to notice them.

As Woman #1 was having her problems, I realized I didn't have the necessary change to operate a copier.

I left my position as next in line and walked to the cashier mentioned previously.

Woman #2 could see me standing at the counter with a ten dollar bill in my hand as I requested change.

At the same time I left my position in line, another man came into the store. He walked by me and assumed the first position in line to use the copiers.

I accepted my fate that I had lost my position in line because I needed change.

When I returned to the line, I stood patiently again, now behind this man. He was much more handsome and younger than I. I could see he only had one copy to make.

The next machine to become available was the one Woman #2 was operating.

Remember, the entire time I was standing in line I believed she had her back to me.

Incredibly now, she turned to me -- the second person in line -- and nodded it was my turn. She knew the other man had assumed the first position in line ahead of me. Instead, she motioned to me with a smile and a slight head bob that she wanted me to step forward. I thought it a kind gesture. I was caught totally by surprised.

The other man, however, aggressively stepped forward. He was ready to make his copy and was not about to relinquish his position in line.

Woman #2 stepped away and caught my eye again and, with a slight tilt of her head, indicated that she had tried on my behalf. I returned her kindness with a smile, a nod of thanks and a slight shrug.

Why had she care at all about me?

What had I done that caused her to want to be kind to me?

In fact, I had no verbal communication with her whatsoever.

But, as you may surmise by now, I had communicated with her. With body language.

Woman #2 must have observed me when I spoke to Woman #1 and tried to help her. Woman #2 also must have seen me when I was standing before the cashier seeking change.

I had used some specific body language before the cashier, hoping to gain faster and better service. Although I didn't think about it at the time, I was standing directly in the view of the Woman #2.

Now I am certain that Woman #2 observed me and was influenced by the male body language I purposely used to get attention and better service from the cashier.

In the brief exchange of body language with Woman #2 when she left her copier, I let her know I appreciated her thoughtfulness. My body language told her it was okay with me that the other man went first.

Finally, consider this about the man who stepped up to the copy machine.

He never once looked at me. As he entered the store, he could see I had to step out of line to get change. He knew I had returned after obtaining the right coins to operate the machine. Despite that, he never made any gesture or concession to me.

This also was observed by Woman #2.

When that man finished, he collected his materials, turned toward the door and marched out. He never indicated he was finished. This would have been a small, polite gesture that many copier users extend to the next person in line.

There is a lesson here for men.

First, body language speaks volumes to other people.

Second, not only did I read the body language of Woman #1, but so did the clerk, the store manager and Woman #2. We all knew she was frustrated, impatient and angry.

Third, Woman #2 went out of her way to extend a courtesy to me, a person she had never met.

Fourth, the man who came in at the end communicated a coldness and an aloofness to both Woman #2 and me. With his body language, this man turned off the same woman who was polite and extended a courtesy to me.

He may have made his copy before me, but I won the kindness of a woman I did not know. His body language was aggressive and assumptive of control and it resulted in one of the worst reactions a man can get from women. His body language spoke loudly, "I don't care about you. I only care about myself." Women respond negatively to that message.

Men exhibit this kind of body language often and cause women to take an instant dislike to them. After reading this book, it shouldn't happen to you.

3.

Reading body language or speaking with it... which is more important to you?

A lot has been written about interpreting body language. Often, you notice articles in men's consumer magazines about reading the body language messages that women send out. The viewpoint of such articles is to help the reader to determine the sexual interest of women they are observing.

How sad this is.

I have read articles like these for years. It is as if, suddenly a woman is like a traffic signal, sending "go" and "stop" signals to men. True, it happens sometimes.

Such articles are of little value to you, if you want to impress women the first time you meet.

You want women to react to you.

You want to intentionally cause a woman to respond to you.

Most men don't know how to use body language to evoke a female response.

It is my opinion that most men do know how to tell if women are interested in them. Articles that appear to share revelations concerning female body language are bogus and absurd. I'm sure if a woman smiled at you, winked at you, began to talk to you, you would take the hint.

Remember this, by the time a woman decides to send out body language signals to you, she already has decided if she is interested in you. To my way of thinking, you have already won the body language battle.

You turned her on.

You made her like you.

Chances are, you'll quickly pick up on her response.

Now, ask yourself this: wouldn't you rather know how to use male body language to intensify her attraction to you?

The more important issue for men today is to know how to use body language to "speak to women." Once you know how, you will easily recognize when women "speak back" to you.

This new language will help you enjoy the benefits of more intense relationships with women. You will know when you are connecting with women for the first time, and you will be able to read their body language responses.

Perhaps your first interpretation of this is in a sexual context. You may see yourself meeting more women and gaining sexual favors. I'm certain that can happen for you under the right circumstances.

I believe your first application of this knowledge of male body language can be applied in business, to influence women in authority.

Today, men are involved in a new role with women in business.

Women have power.

Women hire men.

Women in business are gaining more power everyday.

The converse is that men are losing power in business.

Men are reporting in greater numbers to women.

Many men are becoming subservient to women for the first time.

Not only are men's careers and their employment more dependent on women managers than ever, but also male sales representatives are presenting themselves in far greater numbers to women buyers.

Men must please women in business.

Men must gain the confidence of women managers and women buyers.

Men must convince women business owners that they can work in harmony and carry out assigned responsibilities.

Purposeful use of male body language can help you convey these messages.

One more point about comparing the different abilities to encode versus decode body language.

Reading the body language of women is important in

business. Perhaps, you want to know if your female boss likes your ideas.

Can you make her like you?

Can you get her to give you the best assignments?

Can you encourage her to promote you and move your career ahead?

If you are in sales, perhaps you want persuade women buyers to favor you and your company as one of her frequent vendors.

Can you encourage her to buy your product?

Can you encourage her to put your company on the bid list?

Can you persuade her to approve your proposals, price estimates and sign a contract?

While you can gain insight to what a business woman is thinking by reading female body language, you can influence her decisions by knowing how to use male body language.

The immense power of body language is derived not in decoding it, but encoding it.

It is a little like using a telephone.

If your knowledge of body language only permits you to read the messages that women give off, you are operating a one-way telephone. You can hear, but you can't speak. You can only react to what the speaker is saying; she will not react to you.

Consider this example:

You are in an emergency situation where a phone is your only tool for survival. You are inside a building that is about to be demolished. Dynamite is set and you are on the fourth floor looking out the window. You can see the demolition crew on the ground below getting ready to push the plunger. Indeed, you know that they are doing.

You pick up the phone to make a desperate cry for help and to tell them to stop. In the ear piece, you overhear a conversation. The voice is saying that everyone has evacuated the building.

You want to let the demolition team know their information is wrong. You are still in the building.

There is no mouth piece on the phone.

You can hear them; they cannot hear you.

Without the ability to encode body language, you are in a similar life-and-death business situation today.

Woman determine your fate. If you could persuade them with non-verbal communications, you could change everything for yourself.

This book provides you with techniques that show you how to encode body language that women understand and react to. This book provides you with a "behavior model" that you can use as a starting point to develop body language you will use in your encounters with women.

The purpose of this book is to show what kind of body language to avoid, and what kind to use. When you know this information, you can send signals that women understand and respond to positively.

4.

Women do not like aggression.

Men are aggressive physically.

Some women are aggressive in getting what they want.

However, few women like overt, physical aggression directed at them.

Do you agree?

Think about obvious differences between men and women.

Most men either play or watch hard contact sports such as football and basketball and hockey. In these sports, men run at each other, often at full speed, smashing into other men. Men enjoy these kinds of activities, even though men are often hurt by participating in them.

Some women enjoy sports. Some women are athletic. An increasing number of women are playing highly physical, aggressive contact sports.

Let's be honest, the vast majority of women are not going to take up boxing, wrestling, football or ice hockey as a pastime. They simply would not enjoy it.

In the same way that most women would find it repulsive to be forced to sit and watch men punching, hitting, and striking one another, women are offended by being in the company of a physically aggressive male. This is true, particularly if a male is being overtly aggressive with body language toward them. You will see how men do this shortly.

Please, let me clarify one point:

Women are aggressive. I have known some extremely aggressive women who would steal another woman's husband, try to attract men through any means possible, and would do anything to get ahead in business.

Generally speaking, however, female body language is aggressive in different ways than male body language.

On one hand, women use female body language to attract

others to them. On the other hand, men exhibit body language that is fearsome in nature.

Men, especially aggressive men, use body language constantly that is challenging and confrontational. In the presence of other men, this kind of male body language works. It tells other men, "I am strong. I am without fear. You do not scare me."

Men respond to physical power and respect it. This does not mean that men will cower in the presence of another strong male. Rather, they will not encroach the other man's domain unless they intend to challenge the other male.

Men also like to have strong, aggressive men around them. It is a mistake for men to believe that women like this also.

Consider the camaraderie of men on sports teams at all levels of professional and amateur sports. Weak players -- read this as weak men -- are cut from teams. Only the strongest, most physically talented men get to participate. This encourages men to display their physical powers and abilities.

Part of the problem with male body language is that *men spend the majority of their lives learning how to be successful in the company of other men.* This leads them to exhibit <u>aggressive</u> body language, which is exactly the opposite of what attracts most women.

It's no wonder that many men have no idea what they are doing wrong when they meet a woman. Acting strong and appearing physically dominate works in the presence of men. Men carry this forward when they meet women. They expect the woman will be impressed by their physical strength and appearance. The opposite occurs. Women do not look at them long enough to give these men a chance to talk and dispel the threatening physical appearance they created.

What men don't understand is the message they communicate. With unspoken language, they are saying, "I am bigger and stronger than you are. I can hurt you; you can't hurt me."

An aggressive stance, a powerful posture, and a forceful pose is startling and fearsome to woman. The communication is instantaneous. With few exceptions, the female reaction is predictably negative. It triggers the "flight response" in women.

Men can be far more successful with women once they realize how to control their body language and modify how to display themselves. Men must achieve a different, more inviting message with body language when in the presence of women.

Remember:

• Continue to use your present aggressive body language with men.

• Change your body language when you are in the presence of women.

• In mixed company, use body language attractive to women.

If you are in mixed company (men and women), adopt body language that favors women. Be assured that other men will not be offended. The difference is so subtle that other men will not know. They will not react to you. They will probably be totally unaware that you are standing and sitting differently when women are present.

The reaction you are likely to encounter is that women in the room may choose you to talk to and sit or stand next to you.

What could be better?

The response from other men is likely to be admiration that the women chose you for socializing. Some men may want to know your secret.

5.

Study female body language and what it tells you.

Here is the major difference about women. It also has a lot to do with how women judge men at first glance. This is not a put down to women. It is simply a fact of life.

Women are taught from their earliest years that they should be "pretty" and should display their bodies in attractive ways.

Usually, when an adult meets a little girl for the first time, the initial conversation typically consists of something like:

"Oh, aren't you pretty."

"You have such beautiful eyes."

"What lovely hair you have."

"I like that dress, you look so pretty in it."

Girls receive constant verbal reinforcement about their looks and their appearance. Mothers and fathers reassure little girls that they are pretty.

As girls grow up, they observe women role models being called beautiful and pretty. They are bombarded with advertising messages about beauty and how to achieve it. Think about the clothing and cosmetic industries. Women's magazines overflow with stories, tips, questionnaires and articles on beauty.

I'm not so much commenting on social norms -- whether this is right or wrong -- but I want to make you aware of the impact that this has in the body language differences between men and women.

First, posture plays an important role in female body language.

If you look at women in magazines, on television, in movies, in corporate offices, behind counters, virtually everywhere, you will notice a universal trait about female body language.

Women *display* their bodies.

Women have a special appreciation for and knowledge of how to display their bodies. Men are attracted to women simply by how they stand. They admire the female form. Women learn the importance of standing and sitting in certain ways that flatter themselves from the time that they are young.

"Sit like a lady!"

"Stand up straight!"

"Don't slouch!"

"Don't sit that way, dear, you don't look very pretty."

You can be sure every girl hears these admonishments from parents and teachers. The effect is that women become more attentive to their posture. Consequently, they also notice how others are sitting and standing. As they mature, they find that standing and sitting in certain ways can gain them attention.

I had to smile at the advice that a columnist gave one of her high school cheerleader readers about sometime ago. The girl said that she was taught to stand straight, with a good posture. She had complained that the other girls told her to knock it off because she was attracting so much attention from the boys in school. The columnist advised her not to throw her shoulders back so far. The implication was that this young lady was showing off her ample chest.

This teenage cheerleader knew she had a great body and was using it to her advantage. She was only in high school. I don't doubt that she will use the knowledge about the effects of showing off her breasts all of her life to influence men. After all, she only needs to stand straight and hold her shoulders back. Favors begin coming her way.

Wouldn't it be great if men had the same power? Perhaps you do.

Women learn early on what their best features are.

The young woman above found that her breasts were important to her looks. Could you see her wearing tight sweaters? Vee-neck dresses? Form-fitting coats? Bikini tops? When she wanted to impress someone or get attention, she knew she could do it.

Of course, not all women are gifted in the same way. Women learn to use the gifts they have.

Some women use cosmetics to highlight their best features and cover up their worst. They change the color of their hair and their hair styles to find just the right combination of hue, cut and style to make their hair attractive. I can think of several women I have admired who have strikingly beautiful hair.

As you think about how women are so aware of their bodies and their looks, compare that to what you know about men.

For instance, if you ask a woman about her best facial feature, she will instantly tell you. "It's my eyes," or "It's my cheek bones," or "It's my smile."

Women know themselves.

They would never think to hide their best feature.

Could you imagine asking a man the same question? The guy would go blank.

Here's more to think about.

Concerning their figures, every woman knows the kinds of clothes in which she looks best. I mentioned the cheerleader. She's only one example.

I've often studied how women use information about their figures to their advantage. If a woman has a beautiful neck, she will feature it with necklaces, earrings that dangle with hair up, or brightly colored chokers.

If her breasts are particularly attractive, she will display them in many ways -- with blouses, dresses and jackets that use lines, colors, and patterns to highlight and reveal. Even when such a woman is completed draped from neck to waist, the impression her clothes leave is unmistakable that her breasts are her best feature.

Women with beautiful waistlines have ways to flatter themselves. They wear big, broad belts, often in bright colors. A woman with a beautiful waistline, in fact, is seldom without a belt.

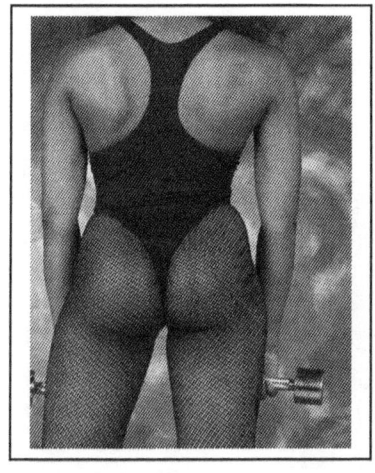

Vice versa: women who dislike their waistlines will never wear a belt or draw attention to their waistlines. They cover up with jackets and flowing blouses and loose fitting dresses.

Women with beautiful buttocks also know how to highlight these features. They wear form-fitting pants and skirts, with tighter cuts.

Women with beautiful legs show them off. They will wear slit skirts, short shorts, tight pants and even ankle bracelets to cause men to look from toe to hem.

Understand these facts and know their impact:

1) Women know their best features.

2) Women know how to highlight their best features.

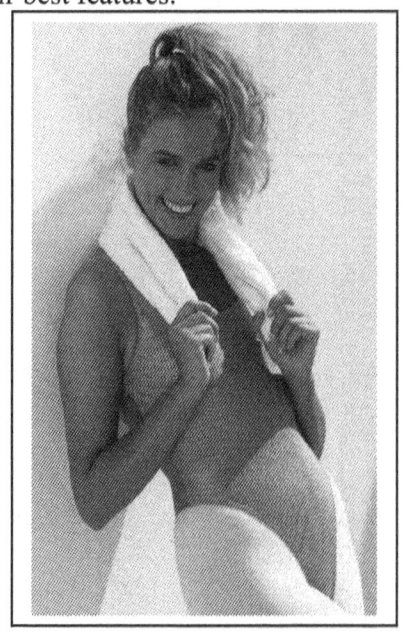

3) Women are encouraged to display their best features.

4) Women display their best features to gain an advantage.

Now, the point.

Display is a passively aggressive act.

I hope you stop here and think for a minute. This is the crux of a key issue. Women are aggressive by displaying an attractive, alluring body. Women use their bodies like magnets. In a sense, they "show you what they've got." They want men to respond.

Put yourself in a woman's position for a minute.

Virtually every day, as a woman, you would get up in the morning and dress for the day. As you get dressed and put on

your make up, you highlight your best features. You try to make yourself pretty and attractive.

Part of your goal in dressing this way is to be pleasing to men and, to a lesser extent, to women. You may envy women who are beautiful and who get what they want simply through their appearance.

When you walk into a room, you want other people to be attracted to you. You want to make heads turn. After all, you were taught as a young girl that being pretty was important. All your life, you've been working at it. Certainly, you are not going to make yourself ugly. You use every bit of knowledge about yourself to look good and present an image that is appealing.

The next key point is: *For a woman to look pretty, she must become physically vulnerable.*

Think about how a woman who is displaying her body must stand and sit.

Women keep their arms at their sides, or behind their backs. They hold their shoulders back. Their are arms are in no position to defend themselves. Often women will stand with one leg in front of the other to make their bodies appear slimmer. They lean and bend in certain ways that accent their bodies.

These positions make them open for a physical attack. They depend on others around them not to attack them, but to look at and admire them.

Women must present themselves in these defenseless positions in order to effectively display their bodies.

On the other hand, men normally do not stand in vulnerable positions. If a man would strike a pose with his arms behind his back among other men, he would be vulnerable to the simplest frontal attack. Such attacks come often when boys are growing up. Being hit is a concern of growing boys and it stays with them through early manhood.

Men know, from experience, that other aggressive men will attack them. That's why men cover up. Men stand in strong, defensive/offensive postures. This makes men appear aggressive.

Men adopt aggressive postures early in life for defensive purposes. It starts during boyhood and adolescence when they are routinely attacked by other aggressive males. Boys wrestle with other boys. They hit and punch one another by surprise and say things like, "Oh, that got you good!" Later, there will be a surprise retaliation.

Males begin hitting each other starting in grade school. It continues through middle school and extends through high school. It's not uncommon for a boy to take a "playful punch" while walking down a hallway between classes. Boys learn always to be ready to defend themselves.

If they look tough and adopt the right postures, they take fewer punches. Boys learn to look aggressive and fearsome. They carry this with them into manhood. A newspaper columnist described how boys can carry body language like this into adulthood. She said men, who are deeply insecure and even afraid of strangers, think they must protect themselves from possible attack. Unconsciously they decide to frighten others away, first with hostile appearances and behavior. They can build a wall or add armor around themselves. This unconscious attitude can prevent such males from fulfilling their potential.

Now, think how a woman, standing in a defenseless position, feels when she meets a man who looks aggressive.

The woman feels vulnerable.

She has been taught to display herself.

The man was taught to look aggressive.

The woman has nothing to protect her body. Her clothing is soft and revealing. She feels she is open to attack.

From the first moment she sees an aggressive male, she senses overt aggressiveness.

She may not know what is making her feel this way.

She knows she is uncomfortable and does not want to be in his presence.

She may be scared and angry all at once.

Instantly, she may become extremely defensive.

The sad part is the man may actually be a nice guy. He was only doing what he was taught. The man believes he is not supposed to appear vulnerable.

When a woman reacts negatively, he has no idea what he has done to cause that reaction. He believes he should be admired for his aggressive appearance. He's stunned by her rejection.

This happens to countless men everyday who unconsciously repel women.

Let me reveal more to you.

This difference between men and women is part of the reason for what we typically call the "battle of the sexes." Men look fierce; women instantly recoil. Women look vulnerable; men appear ready to attack. The language is nonverbal. Much is communicated with body language.

I never used to understand, for instance, why my wife would remark after studying a group of people at a party, "that man is such a hog!"

She would direct these comments toward a strange man who was across the room. I would watch her wrap her arms around her chest, in a protective, hostile reaction. I wondered what she read in his body language that made her feel that way. Today, I have a much better appreciation for her feelings.

Women resent men who stand in aggressive postures.

As for men who want to use body language to their advantage, you must understand this basic point about women. The body postures that women adopt at an early age make them totally helpless in the face of aggression. Women are on display. Their bodies are presented in relaxed, accented ways to cause you to appreciate their best features and respond to them.

To do this, they must show themselves and be vulnerable. Their arms are back. Legs may be crossed, and in positions that are incapable of protection or flight. Even their shoes may look good but lack functional ability for protection or escape.

To be successful in attracting women or predisposing them toward a positive initial reaction, men must not present themselves in a physically aggressive manner.

This means you have to study your body posture and adjust the way you stand, sit and move. You must neutralize your naturally aggressive body language. Don't look threatening. Don't look combative. You want to prevent women from being frightened or repelled by you.

Remember:
- Women are taught to display their bodies.
- To display her body, a woman will
  - hold her arms behind her or at her side.
  - wear delicate and revealing clothing.
  - leave herself open to attack.
  - appear and feel defenseless.
  - react negatively to aggressiveness
- Women feel vulnerable at the slightest aggressive signal.
- Men repel women instantly by appearing to be aggressive.

6.

Study the male posture and see what it tells you.

Men are aggressive in the ways they move, stand and sit --
and this works against them when they are in the presence of
women, particularly when they meet a woman for the first time.

To reveal to you the underpinnings of male posture, look
back to the typical male childhood. Boys play rough and tumble
games. They wrestle, roll around on the ground, punch each
other, push and pull, and use their physical natures to gain the
advantage.

Boys come to understand quickly their ranking in the
pecking order with other boys. They know who is the strongest,
who hits the hardest, who is the best fighter.

I know a boy about ten named Juan. Juan is the best fighter
in his school. He is often challenged, but Juan always wins.
Other boys admire Juan, even though they take a few shots from
this tough, but likable kid from time to time. Some boys also
seek protection from Juan when they are threatened or hurt by
other boys who bully them.

Boys hit other boys regularly. Punches can come at any
time, so a boy learns he must be ready to protect himself at any
moment.

Between the ages of eight and eighteen, boys significantly
change their body postures to protect themselves from bullies.

When boys are little, they are relaxed and vulnerable.

As they grow older, they keep their arms closer to their
bodies. If you make the slightest aggressive move toward a boy
who is about twelve, you will see what I mean. He will respond
by pulling his elbows in. He may aggressively flare his fingers.
He may raise his forearm and turn side ways to catch or deflect a
punch or kick.

Through the years of early adulthood, young men continue this pattern. They move quickly to protect themselves and are constantly alert to danger.

Remember, the kind of situation or social event has little effect on this typical interaction of boys, teenage males or young men. I am sure you can recall witnessing one young male striking another in school, at a social event, during a party or a dance. The attempts to physically dominate and intimidate are constant among young males. For this reason, young men cannot rest in vulnerable positions.

Boys learn defensive postures which can appear to be aggressive. As a youth, a boy learns to keep his feet apart to be able to move quickly for defense. They stand square to you, ready to respond to a challenge. When you observe boys together, you seldom see them in relaxed positions, particularly when they are close together. If you are too relaxed, you invite assault. Another boy might hit you simply because he believes he can get away with it at that moment. This is how boys test each other, and train each other to be aggressive and alert to danger at any moment.

This is all part of the animal nature of humans. Similar behavior can be seen in lion cubs, puppies, bear cubs and other animals, particularly in species that are carnivorous and may be required to hunt other animals to survive.

How aggressive are young males?

About two years ago, I watched a neighborhood boy kick another boy in the groin who was laying on the ground. They had been fighting. The fight seemed to break up, and then the kick was executed. Indeed, I was shocked, but not surprised, by the event. This kind of violence happens to most boys on regular intervals.

Aggressive acts happen to all boys. Confrontations occur on basketball courts, in school lavatories, sledding slopes and swimming holes.

Bigger, stronger aggressive boys constantly attack smaller, weaker ones. To counteract this constant aggression, boys continually learn new, more aggressive ways to stand, sit and move.

Boys and young men use postures and body language to prevent aggression. Their body language says, "I'm ready," and "Don't try it." To stop aggression against them, boys learn to look increasingly more aggressive. From my personal experience and observations, it is the simple truth.

How does this translate into male body language that instantly offends women?

Consider the clash that occurs when one person who is in a vulnerable position-- on display -- is confronted suddenly by a much stronger, bigger person in an aggressive body posture. The result is instantaneous. The woman -- at the first sight of such an aggressive male -- becomes defensive.

There are several responses a woman usually resorts to. She can retreat or flee from the area.

If she feels safe in the location, but does not want the aggressive male to pursue her, she can act disinterested. She may ignore the conversation, or take up a separate conversation with friends nearby.

If she is a business woman, she may politely hear what the male is there to present, and then shorten the meeting. The business woman may make a mental note never to invite that man back into her office again.

A major source of difficulties between men and women is that male aggressive postures, that work so well in the presence of other men, fail miserably in the presence of a woman.

By now, you have a good understanding of the conceptual differences between the body language of typical men and women.

- Women are passively aggressive.
- Women highlight their best features.
- Women display their bodies.
- Women are vulnerable by the ways they sit and stand.
- Women feel threatened in the presence of aggressive males.
- Men learn to appear aggressive.

- Men cover their bodies with protective clothing, even armor.
- Men tend to appear fearsome to women.
- Men can easily scare away women through appearance alone.

7.

Male Body Language To Avoid.

Men are born hunters. It is something in our genetic makeup as carnivores.

I like to reflect on the history of mankind, because the ancient, deep-seated motivators that drove early man to hunt are still inside men today.

The first image that comes to mind of a prehistoric man is that of a hungry survivor, who lived day to day on what he could yield through stalking and killing. You can envision the stone age hunter, standing on a hill, surveying the landscape with his eyes.

He is looking hard, trying to find his prey. Now he sees it. Now he tracks it. Now he moves in for the kill.

Keep this sequence of actions in your mind.

Realize that man first begins to hunt with his eyes. Men began to hunt with their eyes millions of years ago. It is the same today.

Have you ever noticed how women react when you look at them for the first time?

Women can interpret your first look as an aggressive act. Depending on how you do or do not control your eyes, your first look at a woman can cause an immediate defensive action and cause her to repel or flee from you.

"I didn't like the way he looked at me!"

Have you ever heard a woman remark about how she was angered by the way a man looked at her? It is a common remark. Women react negatively to strong, piercing looks that men make with their eyes.

Many men do not even know what they have done. In fact, a man, with no expression on his face, looking passively at a woman, can be interpreted as aggressive by the woman. Women are keenly sensitive to the way men look at them. Any look by a man toward a woman can result in a negative reaction.

Consequently, I have come to realize that men increase their chances of developing a new relationship with a woman by avoiding looking at her.

Let that sink in for a moment. *Avoid looking at women.*

Looking at a woman can be interpreted as aggressive and may turn women off.

You may be wondering how in the world you can get a woman's attention if you do not look at her.

Let me reassure you. It is better that you do not turn off or anger a woman by looking at her if you are ever going to meet her or develop a relationship with her.

Let her notice you.

She will like you much better for it. She will more quickly feel at ease in your presence. She will trust you more, be more relaxed and tend to reveal more about herself to you.

However, if you follow a woman with your eyes, the opposite is likely to occur. She will likely flee your presence. She will be defensive and protective about herself. She will close you off from her private world.

Control your eyes. This is the vital first step to your success in developing relationships with women.

I know that this is paradoxical, given everything I have said about women displaying their bodies. You would think that women want men to look at them and enjoy the beauty they are offering. This is only partially true. The truth is women want only certain men to enjoy their physical display. They "give" permission to certain men. Women believe it is up to them to choose and control which men can enjoy this privilege.

That's why when you walk into the room for the first time and you encounter a woman you do not know, staring at her or taking undue notice of her physical charms can cause you to be rejected instantly by her.

Do you want to test my theory?

The next time you look at a woman you have not met, watch her eye and body movements.

Invariably, her eyes will look away from you. She will deflect your stare. Her eyes will not return your gaze as you look her up and down.

She will not look you in the eye.

She will maintain a certain distance from you. She will probably turn her back to you. She will be unapproachable.

If you meet a woman in a business situation and you look at her in an ogling manner, you are likely to encounter a very negative reaction. Your interview will be short and curt.

If a business woman must sit in the same room with you and you look at her in this manner, she will likely adopt defensive body language. She may fold her arms in front of her. She may ignore you completely and be cool to every remark you make, even the most polite comments. Or, she may show some subtle anger.

Why do men ogle women?

I think it is because of the hunter in our makeup. Men are on the hunt constantly. Women are the prey.

When a man looks at a woman in a certain way even before they are introduced, the woman interprets her role as the prey in this aggressive scene. She does not like it, just as you would not enjoy being hunted. Nor does a woman want to be considered your trophy, your challenge, or your conquest.

How should you handle your eyes?

Avoid looking at women.

This is probably the hardest rule to follow. Men enjoy looking at women. But if you want to be successful in attracting women, you must avoid looking at them initially.

Remember, you will never get to know a woman if she is unwilling to look at you. Instead, you must create a situation in which she will look at you. I will tell you how shortly.

Are you convinced that looking at women causes the opposite reaction you desire? Consider this example:

Here is a typical situation that women abhor: construction workers making catcalls and wolf whistles at women on a sidewalk in New York.

Most women hate this! They consider it demeaning, reducing them to a hunk of flesh that dirty, drooling animals want to slobber over. The construction workers, on the other hand, see a beautiful female body on display and, in an aggressive way, show their appreciation. What is the result?

Women who find themselves in this situation walk faster as part of their flight response. In the future, they might avoid that street entirely, finding another route to their everyday destination.

Women do not like to be looked at by strange men. They also do not like to be looked at too long and too hard under any circumstances.

The lesson is clear. Men must divert their eyes.

When you come into the presence of a woman, take a quick glimpse of the woman. No matter how beautiful she is, always look away before she sees you looking at her. Act disinterested in her beauty. Say nothing to her about her appearance. Make no comments about her clothing, her hair or her style.

Tell her through your body language and eye movements that you would rather focus your attention elsewhere. It is as if to say, "Ah, there is something more interesting over there, away from you."

Let her know from the first moment that you will not stare at her body.

It is far better to give her plenty of opportunity to look at you.

By looking away, you let the woman know that you are not threatening to her. This puts her at ease, and somewhat in control of the situation. It also lets her take her time looking at you.

This is a powerful turnabout which works in a positive manner for you. To cause this to happen, use several techniques.

Concentrate on something else in view.

At social events, I find something on a wall or a table to study with my eyes. I look at the decorations. I might even study the actions of other men. But no matter what I do, I do not look at women in such a way that they will see me looking at them.

In a business situation, I try to become engrossed in a magazine or the annual report in the waiting room. Once in an office or a conference room, I find a photograph, or furniture to look at.

If I see something unusual going on, such as construction or remodeling, I study the work in progress during the free moments that typically occur during breaks in work.

Oddly enough, these kinds of eye techniques can result in exactly the kind of reaction men most desire by the women they meet.

Without looking at a woman, you may find it easier to engage her in conversation. You will find that a woman who believes you are uninterested in her will be friendly toward you.

A good way is to make a simple, off-hand remark about whatever you are looking at. I'll give you some samples in a moment. Try to make your remarks non-aggressive, nor critical.

Simple observations work best, such as:

"That construction work is pretty loud"

"I don't recall seeing that shade of blue in a rug before"

"This is a busy office with all the traffic going through here."

"Everyone looks like they are working hard. How's business?"

"I like the Christmas decorations. They are festive."

You will be surprised by the reaction and the sudden conversation your remark will bring. It may take a second or two. Be patient, and keep looking at what you are looking at. When you first speak, the woman will glance at you and size you up.

She can have one of two reactions. If you are looking at her when you made your remark, she may believe you are simply trying to engage her in conversation. She may see your attempt as a typical male come-on, and give you a one-word answer.

On the other hand, if she believes you are interested in the decorations, the blue rug, the construction -- anything but her --

she is far more likely to become friendly and share her thoughts with you about the subject you raised.

When the woman in your presence feels completely at ease with you, she will make the conversation friendly. She will open up, reveal her feelings and add her observations about the subject.

I have put this theory to the test on numerous occasions, and the results are consistent. I have found more women enjoy talking and will talk longer when they do not feel you are looking at them.

Here's a typical example.

At a party I attended, I wanted to see how many women I could talk to and how long they would talk to me.

I knew I had to find something at the party about which I could make an idle remark. I observed that all the walls were decorated with handmade holiday decorations.

When I found myself standing next to a woman I had not previously met, I casually remarked about how much work had gone into the party decorations. I wasn't looking at her at the time. I was simply standing next to her, and I had my eyes fixed on a display of decorations.

The remark opened up a flood of comments from the woman. She related the entire genesis of the decorations, from the moment they were conceived to the second we were standing there viewing them.

She knew that the hostess had enlisted the aid of her two sons to make the decorations. She told of the fun the family had pasting the decorations into position. She laughed and related several the incidents that had happened while the children were making the decorations. She was completely at ease talking to me.

I glanced at her a couple of times. Mostly, I continued to look from decoration to decoration while she was talking.

It was interesting to note that she tried to look me in the eye several times while she was talking. I would let her catch my eye for a few seconds, then look away. I never looked at her body.

I'm certain that she felt I was sincerely interested in the holiday decorations.

Here is another example of the same technique.

I was shopping at a busy electronics store. After selecting my purchase, the clerk directed me to a payment counter. Three beautiful young women, attractively dressed, were operating the payment center. They were busy and gave me little attention.

Because of the provocative way they dressed -- tight fitting sweaters and blouses, long flowing hair, impeccable makeup -- it was a good guess that men try to engage them in conversation regularly.

I looked away from them after the woman in the center look my credit card. I noticed a row of new television sets, all showing the same feature film. I remembered some research I had read that people in electronics stores work harder if the same repetitive entertainment package is shown over and over on the demonstration televisions.

While looking at the televisions and away from the young women, I made a remark about their enjoying the same show a dozen times each day.

There was a brief silence. Out of the corner of my eye, I saw the woman in the center look to the woman at her right. There was some visual cue between them. I felt they communicated two thoughts. 1) This guy is all right. He's not hitting on us. 2) He's hit a nerve. We really hate watching the same thing over and over.

The woman who was in the center began to talk at length. She described how boring it was to see the same movie continuously.

The woman at her right began talking about how she had memorized the lyrics to all the songs.

Both women began to laugh, and bubble with conversation.

I was still looking away, and glancing back at them from time to time.

Now, I could see they wanted me to look at them. They became animated. The third woman joined in and they started joking even more about the movies. They were sharing private thoughts and comments with me that they had only shared among themselves.

Now I am looking right at them. I'm smiling at them and they are smiling at me.

I'm getting to see these three beautiful women, animated, happy and excited. It was delightful. I was almost sorry my transaction came to an end.

If I had been looking at them at the beginning of this encounter, do you think they would have reacted the same way? Do you think they would have opened up? Or, do you think they would have become defensive and rushed me through the line without saying a word?

Controlling your eyes is vitally important in first encounters.

Use the same approach I described. Find something to look at and make a casual, off-hand remark about it.

The key is not to be aggressive. Instead of looking at a woman, look away from her well before she sees you looking at her.

If you control your eyes, women are more likely to enjoy your company because they will be comfortable in your presence.

Instead of scaring them away with your "hunter" eyes, women will remain calm. Most importantly, you will not immediately trigger a woman's natural instinct to flee or take on a defensive attitude. You are more likely to prevent a reaction that will completely kill your chance at a budding relationship.

Controlling your eyes will give you time to develop a simple strategy to engage a woman in conversation -- one in which she may reveal a great deal about herself to you -- and allow you to begin building a fragile, but positive relationship.

Once the conversation is started, continue to control your eyes. Understand that the woman wants to look at you to evaluate her interest in you. She will do so only if she is unobserved by you.

As a conversation develops, you can begin to make eye contact with her. Do not look at her too hard or too long.

Make certain that you continue to look away often to allow her to relax and feel as if she is not being stared at.

One easy way to do this is to appear as if you are thinking. Many people look away as part of their thinking process. It is a common habit. Watch for it.

If you happen to look back at the woman too quickly and notice she was sizing you up, do not act surprised. Even though you were hoping for this fortunate turn of events, casually look away again, as if you did not notice her looking at you.

One technique is to look away a second time, feigning to think for another moment. You are making progress. If the woman is looking at you, you can feel certain that she is gaining interest in you.

Listen to what she has to say and become involved in her conversation.

Remember, do not be critical.

Provide her with open ended questions that begin with *how, what, when* or *why*. Your goal at this point is to let her talk and continue making conversation with you. In later chapters, I'll tell you how you can use body language to encourage her interest in you.

Remember, control your eyes:
- Do not look at women first.
- Do not undress them with your eyes.
- Do not follow them with your eyes.
- Look at neutral objects, such as decorations, paintings, surroundings.
- Look at activities nearby such as construction, traffic, or other workers.
- Make a simple observation about what you are looking at.
- Give a woman time to respond to your neutral comment.
- Do not look at the woman while you are waiting for her to respond.
- Never say anything about the woman's appearance.
- Avoid all critical or aggressive remarks.

- Continue to look away from the woman after the conversation begins.
- Make limited eye contact so the woman feels completely at ease.
- If you catch her looking at you, look away and give no indication you observed her interest in you or your body.
- Remain casual and relaxed.

If you follow these steps, a woman who has some interest in you will begin to move the conversation forward. She will create opportunities for you to respond to her.

You are on the right track. A fragile relationship is beginning. To nurture it, you must stay relaxed and totally non-aggressive.

If you do, the woman will begin to drive the conversation. Your role is to let her take control and make her feel comfortable.

It will happen if you will remain non-aggressive toward her.

8.

The Approach: Don't Steamroll

Regrettably, twice in one year, I incited the anger of two women simply by the way I approached them. One was my wife.

In each case, I had something completely different on my mind than what my body language spoke loudly to them. I was simply in a hurry. I was rushing to get things done and had wanted to convey a simple message. When I look back now, I know that my approach conveyed the wrong message.

Here's what happened with my wife. While she was out, I noticed that something was wrong in the house. I cannot remember now exactly what it was, perhaps a door had been left unlocked that normally would be checked during the course of the day anyway. I had work on my mind and was rushing to get an assignment done.

As soon as my wife's car pull into the garage, I left my office and met her at the kitchen door.

Remember, I was rushing and I was moving in aggressive ways.

I was taking fast steps toward her.

I was intent on other things, and I knew I only needed to mention that the door was left unlocked.

In my haste, I blurted out what I wanted to say and then started to grab a cup of coffee and return to my office.

Her reaction was instantaneously negative. From her point of view, she saw a man, much bigger than she, rushing toward her.

My head was down, my arms and shoulders were pumping like pistons.

All this male energy was coming right at her.

She immediately became defensive. I can't remember what she yelled at me. It startled me. I had not intended to make a big deal of the door being left unlocked. I did want her to remember to lock it the next time.

I stopped pouring my coffee and stood calmly while she vented her anger. After she cooled down in a moment, I asked, "What did I do?"

"You steamrolled at me," she said angrily. "You charged right at me!"

"I'm sorry," I said, "I've got a lot of work to do and I was in a hurry. I just wanted to make sure you knew about the door, then I wanted to get right back to work."

On a separate occasion, a similar circumstance occurred. Again, it was my fault simply because I walked too fast toward a woman, had something else on my mind, and wanted to keep moving.

There is a lesson here for men, regardless of your familiarity with the woman you are approaching. *Approaching a woman too fast can be intimidating and upsetting.*

Consider yourself to be a big, strong aggressive male -- perhaps in the eyes of women much bigger than you really are. You can appear even more so if you approach a woman too quickly.

When you think about all I have said in this book and how women abhor overt, physical aggression, your approach plays a key role in affecting her attitude toward you. How do you look when you advance toward a woman?

Are you anxious?

Are you breathing heavy?

Is you chest is heaving?

Are your arms and shoulders pumping like pistons in her direction?

Do you look forceful and intent?

The woman can easily assume that she is the target of your intense body motion. She is likely to become upset, even if she does not show it.

Particularly in business, a woman might stand her ground, but be strongly affected by the force of your approach.

If you make such an intense approach toward a woman, by the time you open your mouth to make a comment, a suggestion or pass on a thought, the message might be disregarded.

The first body language impression you made overrided everything you intended to say.

No matter what you utter under these circumstances, it will be viewed as an aggressive statement.

The best way to approach a woman is in a relaxed way.

Take your time coming to her. It might be helpful to control your eyes and look away from her as you approach.

Don't look at her like you are a guided missile electronically locked on your target. It will arouse a negative reaction.

Unless the house is burning down, do not run at a woman.

Do not march toward a woman.

Just walk casually toward her. Smile.

Modulate your voice so you appear calm and this will help her stay calm. It may help to hold your arms at your side, or casually behind your back.

In business situations, use some judgment about your approach. No matter whether you are in charge, or she is, your approach will set a tone.

Of course, the best way to approach a woman is no approach at all. You almost need to be present first, so she can approach you. At the social situation I mentioned in a previous chapter, I parked myself in a location and waited for women to come near me. After they were near me for a while, I made an indirect comment about something I observed.

The woman was free to respond or not respond.

There was no pressure on *her*.

Think how different the reaction is when you walk into a room directly toward a woman. While staring at her, you pronounced, "Gee, they really put a lot of work into these decorations."

What does the woman think?

This guy is trying to come on to me!

He doesn't care about the decorations.

He's very aggressive.

I better find a way to excuse myself; he could be trouble.

There is a big difference when you are far more casual when you approach a woman.

I am reminded of a television commercial for a popular beer. It recaps two points.

A beautiful woman is sitting at a bar, looking at a man a few seats away.

He is not looking at her. The woman finally catches the man's eye and she smiles slightly at him. Her look and smile catch him somewhat by surprise. He looks away, puzzled. So does she.

In another moment, she looks again. He has left his seat. She smiles knowingly. She expects to see him at any second. In another moment, the man is seated next to her. They look at each other, coy smiles cross their faces. End of commercial.

I believe this commercial was written by a woman. It is a beer commercial aimed at women. The star is the woman, not the man.

Notice that the man was not looking at her. He was not being aggressive in any way toward her, particularly with his eyes. When she finally caught his attention, his approach was casual. It was non-confrontational. It was non-aggressive. Suddenly, he is sitting next to her, smiling casually.

Aside from the fact that this is a beer commercial and no matter how unlikely it is that a beautiful woman would be sitting in a bar without men constantly ogling her, the commercial shows a woman's viewpoint of how she would like to meet men and how men should approach a woman.

- The man is not looking at her.
- She attracts the man.
- The man responds in a casual, relaxed way.
- There is not one aggressive move on the part of the man - not with his eyes, his approach, nor his body language.
- She is comfortable when the man is not aggressive.

Remember this always: women are more likely to be comfortable with you when you are completely non-aggressive. This is an essential lesson of Male Body Language That Attracts Women.

When you approach a woman:
- Appear casual and relaxed.
- Do not approach too fast.
- Do not frown when approaching a woman.
- Do not tilt your head down and forward.
- Keep your hands to your sides or behind your back.
- Give the woman time to acknowledge your presence.
- If you must interrupt her, do it politely.
- Control your eyes when you first speak.
- Look away casually to give the woman a chance to look at you.
- Continue to control your eyes after the conversation begins.

9.

Standing in the presence of a woman.

Your stance is something that women respond to strongly. If you stand certain ways, you can repel women. If you control your body movements and positions, you can neutralize any negative reaction, and potentially create a positive attraction.

There are two kinds of poses that irritate women: aggressive postures and disinterested postures.

Aggressive postures attempt to dominate women. Women respond as if they are being intimidated and threatened.

Disinterested postures cause a woman to feel she is unimportant and that there is nothing she could say or do that would interest you.

Posture starts with how you position your feet...how you hold your legs...how straight you keep your back...and the angles of your shoulders, neck and head.

Your feet are your foundation and have an enormous impact on your entire body. Given the fact that most men learn to be highly aggressive as they grow up, one of the things they learn is to plant their feet squarely. This means that the toes of both feet are pointed straight ahead. This is aggressive.

Women can react negatively to this stance, particularly if your standing position is coupled with arm movements or arm positions that connote aggressiveness. Here is an example of a threatening standing position.

Arabian Nights -- Avoid It!
Women can react negatively to this standing position, yet men use it all the time. I call it the Arabian Nights.

Your feet are squared straight ahead; your arms are folded across your chest. Your shoulders are leaning forward naturally when your toes are in this position. You appear to be standing completely erect, and angled slightly forward.

This position can convey a sense of towering power, aggressively angled and ready for combat.

To a woman, you may appear impenetrable. There is nothing about you in this position that attracts a women.

Rather, you appear to be trying to dominating the person in front of you. I call this position the Arabian Nights because it always makes me think of an Arab sentry, sword in sash, standing guard around the harem's tent. It is an awesome, physical display of strength, intended to frighten to all comers.

Do you stand this way often?

Do you stand in similar postures in front of women, towering over them?

While you are standing in these positions, how do you feel?

Do you feel forceful?

Do you feel angry?

Do you want your wishes to be carried out?

Are you resentful of some actions or words the woman said?

If you answered yes to any of these questions, I can assure you that your body language communicated those thoughts to the woman. If it was not your intention to communicate anger, strength and intensity of your will, be advised that your body language betrayed your intentions.

In dealing with women, you should eliminate body language such as Arabian Nights. It can interfere with the objectives you are trying to achieve with your verbal communications.

For instance, say you are in a business situation and involved in sensitive negotiations with a woman manager. Perhaps you are in sales, or making an internal presentation.

You realize you must make concessions in order to obtain her approval. You are willing to do so. At the end of the meeting, you are standing before her. You feel you are close to having a meeting of the minds.

She raises objections that need to be discussed.

You fold your arms across your chest, stand square to her and tilt your head down at her. You appear to glare at her.

Actually, you are thinking about what you are going to say next. You want to phrase your answer to make a concession, but you don't want to go too far.

The woman becomes more intense in her argument.

You frown. The intensity of your negative posture increases.

She raises her voice a little.

You are wondering why she is getting angry. You want to make concessions. You want to make the deal and gain her approval. You are trying to be on her side.

You tighten your arms. You breathe a little heavier, and your chest expands. You feel yourself getting angry. Your voice gets a little louder. You appear more dominating.

She talks faster. Her body language tells you she is angry.

You see all your hard work evaporating. There is no way you can save the deal now.

What went wrong and how can you fix it?

Change your body language so that you neutralize the unspoken messages you are sending to women, stay calm, looked relax and negotiate on the issues.

The Side-Step Position -- Use It.
When you stand before a woman, you can modify your posture significantly by making two small moves to take advantage of the side-step position.

- Point the toes of one foot to the side.

- Drop your arms to your sides, or rest them behind your back.

It is a good idea to try this stance now. It will help you feel the effect of changing your standing position to the one described here.

Start by standing with toes straight ahead. Now, point the toes on your right foot to the right side slightly.

Keep the left foot pointing straight ahead.

Fold your hands behind your back in a relaxed manner.

Here's what happens. As you point your right foot to the right side, you'll notice a shift in your hips, shoulders and head. The amount of shift depends the how wide an angle you open your stance.

As you turn the toes on your right foot to the side, you should feel:

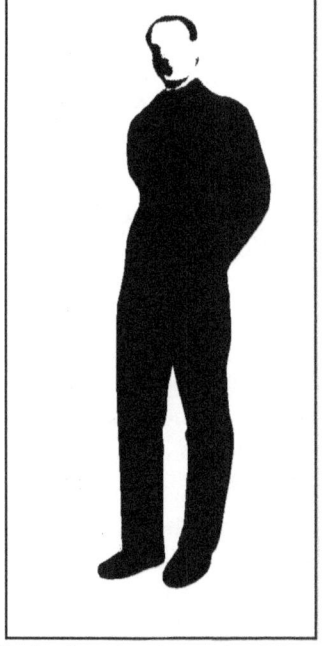

- Your shoulders ease backwards.
- Your head comes up.
- Your shoulders relax and tilt backwards.
- Your chest sticks out a little more.

As you fold your hands behind your back, your shoulders come back and your chest becomes more prominent.

By making these changes, you will tend to stand more erect and taller. You will also appear more relaxed. You will not appear to be dominating the person before you because your head and shoulders fall farther backward. Your body language is less aggressive.

Hiding your hands behind your back is one of the key positions to remember.

Continue to open your stance by moving your right foot a little behind your left foot. As you do by an inch or more, the shifting of your shoulders and head will increase. Your pelvic area may move forward slightly to hold your balance. Remember, keep your hands folded behind your back. You will appear to be less combative and less aggressive.

In this position, your body language is neutralized so it gives off no physical aggressive messages.

This position can also be provocative for a woman. You are giving her a full frontal view of your body.

Thinking about the position of your feet can also help you highlight your buttocks. When you lean backwards slightly on one foot:

- your buttocks will protrude a little more prominently
- you will create a defining line where your buttocks meets the back of your leg.

This is pleasing to women and presents male body lines that women can visually appreciate.

Ramrod Straight Position -- Avoid it.

For a moment, compare this position to the "ramrod straight" position that is often suggested in leadership seminars. To achieve the ramrod straight position, stand with your back against a wall. Your heels, buttocks, small of your back, shoulders and head should all be touching the wall.

Now imagine a woman standing before you. Unless your line of sight is straight with hers, you will be looking down at her. You feel powerful. You are ready to dominate.

How does the woman feel encountering such a male? My advice is to reserve the ramrod straight position for public speaking if you intend to become a dynamic leader. Otherwise, use the "side step" stance for all your interpersonal communications with women.

By adopting "side step" stance, you are actually more physically vulnerable, especially in the pelvic area. Think about the significance of this.

The lines of entire pelvic area are slightly accented.

By pointing one of your feet to the side and shifting one foot backward, your pelvic area moves forward a little.

This shifting takes away some of the natural protection of your genital area that you gained by keeping your feet tightly together. Your genitals are no longer tucked in and protected.

Men are taught to avoid this position as they grow up because they are more vulnerable to attack. Just about every man I know fears being "hit or kicked in the balls."

On the other hand, understand that women are naturally attracted to men, in a manner that is similar to the male attraction to women. Men tend to focus on female body areas.

Given the same opportunity to do so, women are attracted to male body areas. The proof is the incredible and growing popularity of male strippers. Women are delighted to see a man strip, wiggle, gyrate and grind. Women squeal when the tuck money into male stripper G-strings.

The body stance I have described subtly places a man's pelvic and genital areas on display. This should not be misinterpreted as a gross, overt display of your genital area.

You are simply gaining a natural effect of casual lines caused when your pelvic area is slightly forward, as caused by moving your toes wider apart and shifting one foot slightly behind the other.

Standing with square toes virtually hides or almost totally obscures your pelvic area. As you display your pelvic area, and you will find you gain two advantages: you are less aggressive in your appearance, and you are more provocative to women.

This brings up another position to avoid called praying hands.

Praying Hands Position: Avoid It.

Praying hands is the practice of folding your hands over your genital area while you are standing or sitting. Every time I see a man this way I immediately think he is insecure. I wonder, "What is going through his mind?" Is he thinking:

"I feel like a little boy."

"I don't want anyone to look at my dick."

"I've got so much to show, it will get people excited."

"I'm embarrassed."

"I've got an enormous erection and I have to hide it."

"Oh, god, I just wet my pants."

"If I move my hands, no one will pay attention to what I have to say."

There is an element of truth in each of these comments.

Yet, there is no reason for a grown man to cover his genital area with praying hands. It is a distraction which takes away from his maturity and makes him appear lesser than he is.

If you resort to praying hands because you do not know what to do with your hands, try folding them behind your back. Place them on your hips. Put your hands in your jacket pockets. No matter what location you decide to move your hands, make sure you keep them away from the front of your body.

Don't worry: people will not stare at your pants.

The new, more open presentation of your pelvic area in a casual, slightly restrain way will help you gain the notice of many women.

This is not to say that women will gawk at you. But they will take look, every so casually, more often at you. Standing in this new, non-aggressive position shows you are making yourself vulnerable.

You will be displaying your body much in the same manner that women display theirs. Remember, women have been taught all their lives to display their breasts, waists, legs, buttocks and thighs.

One of the men who has learned about these techniques reported back that he observed the display of several women at a party. Two women in particular drew his attention. They both had shapely breasts. They were both dressed in clothing that accented their best features with fairly tight, form-fitting attire.

During the course of four hours at this social engagement, he reported neither woman crossed her arms in front of her breasts. They kept their breasts well in view and did not obstruct this visual presentation with folded arms.

Think about these women and how they displayed themselves.

Display Your Body Lines.

It is perfectly natural and acceptable in our society to display your body. You should think about the lines of your body, and try to match yourself to what I consider the ideal for men today.

I call this model "two bumps and a caboose."

The two bumps are the curved lines that break the vertical plane of the front of your body. The first bump is your chest; the second is your genital area. When you stand, strive to create slight bumps in both these areas. Obviously, a bulging stomach detracts from the attractive curves and lines of the front of the male body.

The caboose is your buttocks, and it should be prominent jutting rounded curves, best shown off in tighter pants, not loose or baggy. Women today are looking more at male buns. The way to accent your caboose is to balance on the heel of one foot, instead of your toes. This helps create an accent line at the bottom of your buttocks where they meet the back of thighs.

Standing in ways that creates prominent or slight lines through your chest and pelvic areas is important to increase your attractiveness to women. Never think that the issue is whether you have a lot or a little to show.

Remember, men notice women of all sizes and shapes who display themselves. The men who are attracted to specific shapes and sizes respond naturally when they see those shapes. *Women will respond to you in the same manner.*

The good thing is that women who are not particularly attracted to your special shape and size will not think any less of you for displaying yourself.

Incredibly, they will think more of you.

They will appreciate that you are one of the few men they see who has enough confidence in himself to causally display his body. They get to look at you and decide for themselves if they like what they are seeing. They feel no pressure, no intimidating tactics, no aggression.

Here are the essential points to remember when you are standing in the presence of women:

- Stand erect, but in a casual way.
- Keep your hands to your sides, or, even better, behind you.
- Open your stance by pointing your toes to a side.
- Put one foot slightly behind the other, shift your weight to your heel.
- Let your shoulders fall backwards.
- Allow your chest to show prominently.
- Create lines along your buttocks by leaning backwards slightly.
- Create lines along the front of your pelvic area by opening your stance.

If you are uncomfortable with your body, please consider building your confidence with a personal exercise program.

The human body is intended to provide beauty and enjoyment to the opposite sex. Your body can work like a magnet to attract women, if only you will allow its beauty to show.

Do not be ashamed.

Although this discussion included some graphic detail, it is likely that the body lines and images discussed here, as applied to you, will not create a dramatic, strongly sexual profile.

Rather, the image you create by changing your stance is subtly different from the one you exhibit now. By making these changes, women will respond by being more relaxed in your presence.

When you do not appear to be aggressive, women can take control of situations. This means they will be more aggressive in leading you in conversations.

When you change your body posture, you also give women more reasons to look at you, and to study the lines of your body. You will be reversing the tables on them, and taking advantage of the same powerful attraction that has caused men to respond to the appearance of women for centuries.

When women are glancing at your clothing lines, you can be sure they are curious as to what is underneath.

10.

Displaying your torso.

Your chest can be your most important feature. You can use it to your advantage when you are seated.

I have spent a great deal of time studying men and women. I often think of the following comparison and reversal of roles.

As a person who has been in many corporate offices and managerial positions for over twenty years, I have a keen sense for the way women are received by men. I am often reminded of my early days as a manager in a large chemical company.

At that time, there were few women in positions of authority. Most women held secretarial positions. The creative services department was an exception. We had two women buyers. As I recall, there was only one senior woman manager in the entire billion-dollar company -- an incredible thought as compared to today's corporations.

Invariably, the secretaries who were promoted and received raises were the best lookers. Think how the promotion system worked for women.

Women were seated hour after hour, either behind their desks or in their bosses' offices. They had to make the best impression from the waist up. These women used clothing, color and style to highlight and outline their breasts.

That era is gone.

Today, few women overtly reveal or highlight their breasts in the same manner as they once did.

Today, the tables are turned. There is an increasing attention to men's pecks. Many television commercials feature shirtless men, their chests rippling with muscles. It's hard not to notice how men's chests have gained so much attention.

Before I go on, I want to draw your attention to another situation. Two years ago, I was with a male friend in his office. He was about to get married. This fellow, in his early thirties, had been lifting weights for years. He had a big chest for his size. His pecks were fairly full, firm and stood high on his chest.

While I was at his office on a cold, wintry day, I noticed that he was wearing a white shirt with no undershirt underneath. His pecks were prominent.

A woman entered his office and interrupted our meeting.

When she came in, he leaned back. This motion resulted in a pose that tightened his shirt across his chest, providing a pronounced presentation of his pecks. The woman was cordial, warm and friendly during the encounter. She presented the work directly to him and smiled broadly at him. Very casually, she had glanced at his chest once or twice. Her glances were not overt.

In a moment or two she was gone.

My friend knew he had prominently displayed his chest for her. It was meant to influence her attitude. It was working. After all, she brought his work right to his desk. She didn't drop the papers into his in-basket, but presented the work directly to him. All he had to do was flex is chest.

I made no mention of my observation, but I did ask my friend afterward if all the women in his office liked him.

He answered simply, "Very definitely," and he smiled a broad smile.

He used his chest in a positive way in a seated position. He did not cross his arms to cover his chest or hide the view of his torso. Instead, he opened his arms, placed his hands on the edge of his desk and pushed his body backwards. Weight lifters will recognize this as a modified press. When you push your hands, palms down, against the desk, your chest tightens and flexes.

You can flex your chest in this natural, relaxed way so that no one notices you are doing it. The key is to act like you are thinking about something else, and this is part of your ritual when you think. Take a deep breath, move your hands into position along the edge of the desk, and exert pressure. Pause, hold the position, look away as if you are thinking. To gain the full effect, you must look away so that the woman present will have time to admire your display. Slowly look back in a second or two. Give your response to the conversation after she has had time to admire you.

When you follow these steps, no one will know you did it.

You can make the same moves to display your chest in a meeting room. Use the edge of the conference table, or use the arm rests on the chair. Make sure you look away while you are doing it as if you are thinking. Pause and reflect for a moment, then slowly look back.

My friend was an expert at putting himself on display. I'm sure it was intentional. I'm convinced it was a secret move he developed over many years. He knew how to highlight his best feature. It worked for him.

Chest moves can work for you, too. It doesn't matter what your measurements are. Your body is naturally attractive to women. If you flex your chest, they will look.

It's human nature to look at the body of the opposite sex.

Reverse the roles for a moment and think how you would react if a woman sat before you and suddenly stretched to get something off a shelf or reached behind her. She would present her breasts to you and you would look, even for the slightest moment.

If she was an exceedingly attractive woman, you might lose your breath.

If she was a normally attractive woman, you would also have a memorable image in your mind.

Even if she was slightly built, you would look and think about her body.

Her image would stay with you. She would affect the way you thought of her because of the way she displayed her body.

• If she was attractive, would you want to be in her presence again?

• Would you enjoy seeing her stretch again?

• Might you try to re-create the same circumstance to see her stretch again?

If you have any male hormones in you, you would answer yes to these questions.

Take this thought one step further.

Let's say that several women visit your office during the course of a week. One or two of these women always "look good" to you.

You want these women in your office more often because they stand a certain way, wear their clothes a certain way, move a certain way.

Perhaps you don't know exactly what it is about these women that attracts you because what they are doing is very subtle.

I can tell you that these women are displaying their bodies in ways that help you appreciate their best features.

Given this to be true, you would most likely be predisposed toward these women whenever they enter your office. The women who display their bodies to you will get more of your attention, no matter what the circumstances.

Women will react to your male body displays the same way.

You can stimulate positive reactions in women. You can stand, sit and move in such ways as to highlight your best features and give women pleasure when they look at you.

You can attract women to you.

You can make them enjoy having you walk into their offices.

You can cause them to set aside time to see you and be with you.

You can gain time on their calendars, and more easily make appointments with them.

Women will want you to be in their presence and they will look forward to your calls.

If you deal with women in superior positions in business or women buyers, or want to be more attractive socially to women, keep these thoughts in mind:

- Display your torso, do not hide it.

- Give women a chance to look at your body by controlling your eyes.
  - Never hide your chest by folding your arms.
  - Be vulnerable and open with your body postures.
  - Find ways to move your arms to accent your chest.
  - No matter what you've got, women want to see it.

Women appreciate that you have put your pecks on display and they will let you know.

In business, they will involve you in more projects and assignments.

If you are in sales, they will want you to come back to discuss bids or to award more work to you.

In social settings, they will want to be in your presence.

They may come over to talk with you at parties or social engagements.

They would rather be near you, and enjoy what they are seeing, than be dealing with a sloppy, lumpy man who exhibits a disagreeable and aggressive attitude.

With the posture described in this chapter, you will be saying to women, "You can look at me. I hope you enjoy what you are seeing. I'm here to make you feel comfortable looking at me."

Not all women will respond positively. Many women will. You will enjoy the benefits.

11.

How to sit provocatively.

Male Body Language That Attracts Women includes a number of sitting positions, which can be combined with hand motions, to influence how women feel about you.

First, let me tell you how NOT to sit.

Sitting With Legs Wide Apart -- Avoid It.

Typical male sitting postures involve legs spread wide apart, feet flat on the floor. This is naturally comfortable for men. Your genitals have more space. They remain cooler than the rest of the body, which is a natural requirement for the reproductive glands.

But you must remember this.

Women do not want to look at you when you are sitting in positions with your legs spread wide apart.

You are presenting a gross portrait to women in this position, with your genital area so openly exposed. This sitting posture will naturally deflect a woman's view. It may cause her to want to leave the room.

How do I know? Put yourself in the position of sitting across from a woman with her legs spread wide apart. Your eyes want to look at her crotch. Your mind tells you that is impolite. You are constantly fighting inside yourself to look, or not to look.

If you were looking at an unattractive woman, her

position would heighten your negative feelings. You might leave, unless you are compelled to stay.

Understand that women have the same feelings when you sit before them with your legs spread.

When men sit with their legs wide apart, they often rest their arms on their legs. It causes them to slouch forward. This can make you appear either an aggressive man, hunkered down, jutting forward in a gross sexual display, or an uncaring man, lazily paying little attention.

You should avoid these sitting position because of the negative messages they send.

A second typical male sitting position is with his legs crossed. There are two ways to sit with your legs crossed. One is highly provocative and flattering to the male form. The other results in a negative impression.

Sitting With Your Legs Loosely Crossed -- Avoid It.

Sitting with your loosely legs crossed can be unattractive to women if your cross your top leg by resting the ankle over the other knee. The result of this loose crossing is that your genital area is still exposed, just as if you had your legs spread wide. Women don't want to look at you when you grossly display your genital area in this manner.

Now, here are some tips about sitting postures.

Sitting With Your Legs Tightly Crossed -- Highly Recommended.

It is more effective to cross your legs tightly.

It can improve the display of your torso. As your body moves backward, it will naturally reveal your chest.

Your head will also tilt backward slightly, helping to reduce an aggressive appearance.

It also significantly improves the display of your genital area, making you highly provocative and attractive to women.

Here is how to sit with your legs tightly crossed:

• Knees should be locked together; one on top of the other, if possible.

- It is also acceptable to extend your legs, keeping the knees together and crossing your legs at the ankles.
- Arch your back to accent your chest.
- Relax your neck and head.

I would not be surprised if you are initially uncomfortable in this position. It is somewhat unnatural to men. It can squeeze the genitals between the thighs.

You will find that you can sit comfortably if your genitals move above your thighs. When your genitals rest on your thighs, this sitting position works like magic. One key advantage is that you will present your body in one of the most attractive displays for women.

Women respond to this male sitting position in remarkable ways. They become animated, chatter, excited and bubbly. They smile a lot. They change their minds to agree with you. They become aggressive in liking you. They may start to touch you, laugh louder and seem stimulated.

If you forget everything else in this book, remember to sit with your legs tightly crossed, and openly display the lines of your genital area.

Do not spoil this display by cupping your hands over your genital area.

Crossing your legs tightly is agreeable and acceptable to women and will cause them to look at you more. Oblige them, and don't spoil the view by hiding yourself with your hands.

This position works well in social and business situations for several reasons.

- It presents you in a relaxed, attentive manner.
- You appear non aggressive.
- It allows you to display your torso and pelvic areas in provocative ways.
- If you lean back to take a breath or to stretch, you will enhance the display of your chest so it is attractive to women.
- Remember to keep your hands at your sides, on the arm rests of the chair, and otherwise away from the front of you.
- You can heighten sexual awareness and response while in this seated position.

Stimulating sexual interest while sitting

While you are sitting in the tightly crossed leg position, you can send sexual messages to heighten female response to you. This can work well to stimulate your wife, your lover, or women you meet in business or socially. They won't even know you are doing it.

To heighten female sexual response, re-cross your legs in the opposite direction from time to time.

Each time you do, you will find that your genitals may move a little higher on the opposite thigh. This will cause them to be displayed more.

Be careful about this.

You may want to avoid over stimulation in a business encounter. On the other hand, if you have some sexual interest in a women that you meet in a business or social situation, this body language can have a powerful effect to excite her.

By moving your legs and increasing the display of your genitals, you may increase her sexual arousal as well as your own.

The key is for you to remain totally non aggressive in all other body language. No matter what else you do, do not indicate in any overt way that you are displaying your genitals more prominently. Let her react to you. Watch her responses and go with them.

It is important while you are shifting and moving to diligently control your eyes. Constantly look away from her. Use the mannerisms described earlier that indicate your are thinking and formulating your words for your conversation with her.

As you re-cross your legs while you are looking away, unconsciously the woman be looking at your genital area. The motion of your legs crossing will cause her to look.

As she glances at you, she will be receiving non-verbal messages that may stimulate her sexually.

One of the messages she may perceive is that you are getting excited being in *her* presence. She may notice that your genital area is becoming more prominent.

What if she thinks she is causing this effect? It could be flattering to her.

Vitally important is that you appear to her as if you are trying to maintain control of yourself. By keeping your legs crossed tightly and looking away from her, you are sending a non-verbal message that you trying to control yourself.

As she observes your physical stimulation, she may believe that she has the power to sexually stimulate you. You are leading her to believe she is in control and is causing this stimulation.

You can push this situation further. Twist your free foot, slowly rotating the ankle. Move your knee, gently. Casually rock and move your body. Make it appear as if you body if filled with energy, so much so that you need to release it. Do so in a highly controlled manner, consistent with the careful image you are building of attempting to constrain yourself. Continue to look away as appropriate.

If you want to heighten her awareness of your genital area, place your hands on your hips, preferably not in your pockets, with thumbs resting in the creases of your lap and point at your genitals. Tap your thumbs occasionally during conversation while drawing attention toward your 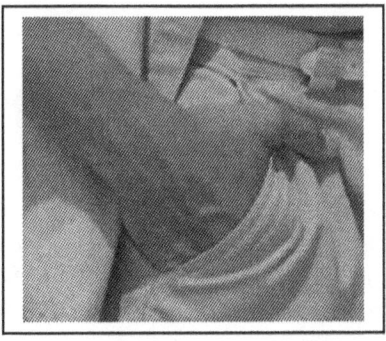 genitals. Time your actions so that whenever you tap your thumbs, you are looking away from her. This creates an opportunity for her eyes to be drawn unconsciously to your genital area.

If you are doing all these things during the course of an encounter that lasts twenty minutes or more, the woman has looked at your body many times. Even if she is in complete control and businesslike, she is human. She unconsciously has become keenly aware of your body, and in particular, your genital area.

What kind of response can you expect?

Observe if the woman:

- Becomes animated, moving her hands, arms and head when she talks.
- Quickens her voice, modulates her tone, sounds more pleasing, conciliatory or inviting.
- Smiles more.
- Leads the conversation.
- Touches you.
- Grips your forearm or thigh during conversation.

If you see any of these signs, you are observing female body language responses. These non-verbal signals tell you she is enjoying the display you are creating.

Continue doing what you are doing. In a business situation, you know you have made a connection on highly personal level. This woman will want to see you again. She may never know why she was so stimulated. But she will remember you turned her on and will want you back in her office again.

In a personal, social encounter, you are connecting on a physical level and the woman is interested in you.

If you are in a private place -- perhaps having an intimate dinner, at your place or her apartment, or watching a show together, you both may become highly sexually stimulated.

If you follow these body language suggestions, you may cause strong sexual desire in her. She will take the lead. It is important that you let her do so. Her touching will become stronger and suggestive. Respond to her and she is likely to take you right to the point you desire most.

Give her plenty of time to look at you. Use these techniques:

1) Look away often.
2) Look back slowly.
3) Do not catch her looking at you.

4) Continue the conversation without giving a clue that you know you are sexually stimulated.

4) Give her no indication that this stimulation and display is intentional on your part.

Continue to let her lead and control events and see where this brings you. No matter what the outcome of this encounter, a woman who enjoyed your display will always think positively of you. Look for her to be more aggressive, friendly and positive toward you in your future encounters. Use these same techniques, as appropriate, the next time you meet. She may eventually find herself irresistibly being driven closer to you.

Here are the key points to remember:

• Sit with your thighs together, knees crossed at either the ankles or knees.

• Cause your genitals to be slightly prominent; rest them on your thighs.

• Look away often and casually so the woman can look at you.

• Pat or rub your thighs to cause the woman to glance at your genital area.

• Move your free foot slowly, twisting your ankle.

• Rock occasionally.

• Stretch backward, take a deep casual breath and display your chest.

• Don't rush or lead the woman to respond because that would be viewed as aggressive.

• If the woman becomes more talkative or animated, or smiles, laughs, or touches you, or becomes more open in her discussion, your display is having an effect.

• As the woman becomes more excited, relax and follow her lead. Let her know you are interested in anything that's on her mind. Continue to use your body language techniques

Once you notice a woman responding to your body language displays, she will remember you fondly. She may bring the same emotional intensity to your next encounter.

Be aware, too, that these sitting positions, when properly executed, can lead to heightened sexual arousal, both for her and *for you* as well.

You may not want this to happen.

To see what I mean, reverse roles for a moment.

Consider a young, attractive secretary using an intense female display to influence her fifty-year-old boss. She may want to get a raise, take an extra day off, or earn another special perk.

On the other hand, she would have problems if the older man made advances toward her, asked her for dinner, or told her they needed to take a business trip together. She may get more than she bargained for by displaying so much and so intensely.

If you are a younger man, you may find yourself in a similar situation with an older woman executive. What would you do when she starts to come on to you? It is easy to light a forest fire; much harder to put it out.

One helpful way of thinking of these body language techniques is to view them as the language of human physical desire. Understand that using these techniques creates a dialogue deep inside the woman receiving these non-verbal communications.

When you use these techniques with women you have no sexual interest in, use them sparingly. You want to arouse the woman just enough to gain your purposes, whether it be to do better in business, or gain a social advantage.

When you use these techniques with a woman who you have a sexual interest in, your intent is different: sexual satisfaction.

Remember, not all women will respond to you. You want to find the responders.

One last suggestion: use these techniques in every situation with women. I find it interesting to use these techniques in business. I particularly enjoy situations in which I deal with hard-boiled women executives. While they are barking orders, demanding services, complaining about strategies or approaches, I cross my legs tightly and slowly rotate my free foot. Occasionally, I will take a deep breath and display my chest.

Throughout their tirades, I continue to send deeply physical non-verbal signals. I wait for the response. Invariably, a positive response comes. I am assigned the project; the woman approves the work promptly, and I get paid my price quickly. In business, you can't do better than that.

12.

Giving up control is a big part of your success.

Do you always like to be in control? This will work against you when you are making new relationships with women.

In experimenting with male body language, I have found that you must give up a measure of control in order to succeed in new relationships with women.

Here's why.

You want to make a woman feel comfortable. To do so, she must lead you.

In reviewing the techniques discussed so far, there is an underlying message here for men. Your control comes from displaying your body so that you attract women. That's where your control ends.

You have no control over which women will be attracted to you. You have no control over what their agendas for you are.

When you use Male Body Language That Attracts Women, women who respond to you will act and feel as if they are in control. You have to "go with flow."

Remember that the woman is interpreting the body language messages. The non-verbal signals she is receiving will tell her: 1) This man in front of me is getting excited and I am stimulating him; and, 2) He is a good man because he is trying hard to control himself. 3) He is non aggressive and trying to do the right thing.

These messages lead the woman to believe that she is in control. It flatters her ego that she could cause such an intense reaction. It is likely that she has not see a man react this way for a long time, perhaps for years. She is unconsciously enjoying it. She is getting sexual pleasure from watching. In her mind, she is a potent stimulant and she can decide how far this situation should go.

You have ignited her fuse.

Now that it is smoldering, the fuse is burning on its timetable, not yours.

If you play your role correctly, the fuse will keep burning.

Eventually, the dynamite will go off.

By intensifying your body language, you may superheat the fuse.

If you halt your body language after the fuse is lighted, the fuse may continue to burn. Watch out! That dynamite can still go off!

Which women will respond to you?

You never know. Be ready for women to approach you at parties and in business situations.

You cannot predict when they will.

You cannot predict what these women will say.

You cannot control the dynamics of the situation.

You must accept that these women have their own ideas and expectations. They will soon let you know.

It is truly amazing that you find out much more about women using these techniques. They will reveal their personalities to you more quickly and will display their bodies more readily.

It is a little like getting into a car in which a new woman you meet is driving. *They take you where they are going.* They lead you.

My advice is to relax and be casual. You can always stop the budding relationship at any moment, if you want to make a clean break.

Some men who read this book will have a strong desire to attract a specific woman. It might be the secretary in the next department, a clerk at the grocery store, your best friend's sister, the widow at church. There are no promises that she will respond to you.

Do not despair. Other women will. When they do, you will appreciate the desire they express to you. You will find you have little time for women who are disinterested in you. There will be so many more who are interested in you.

Here is a typical situation.

You enter a room and notice a woman. You are interested in her. You do not look at her and pay no attention to her. Instead, stand in the side-step position as was described in previous chapters. Begin to observe anything that catches your attention. In the back of your mind, you want the first woman you saw to approach you. If she doesn't, be patient.

Perhaps a second woman will step close to you. If so, focus your body language toward her. Turn your body so she can see a profile of your torso and pelvic lines. She will have more to look at if you clasp your hands behind your back.

Comment about the object or event you are watching.

If the second woman responds, nurture the conversation by encouraging her to tell you what she knows about the object you are studying. Use open ended questions that begin with what, where, why and how.

Let her lead the conversation. Enjoy listening and drawing her out. The less you say, the greater the chance of success. Ask questions and listen to her answers.

Relax, enjoy whatever moments she shares with you. Be patient. You do not know where this will lead.

Eventually, the first woman may take notice of you, too.

Think about how much more she knows about you. Certainly, she observed you in conversation with another woman.

She also took in your non-verbal body language.

She may have been influenced by you more than you know as she observed your interaction with another woman.

Being approached by the second woman could have been a blessing in disguise. Your conversations -- both verbal and non-verbal -- may have given the first woman the courage and desire to want to meet you.

The situation I described is real.

At a recent event, the first woman who engaged me in conversation was not particularly attractive. She was a little overweight and she had strong facial features. I went with it.

She talked to me for about an hour. I enjoyed the conversation; she owned a business and told me some fascinating stories about a family power struggle. After about an hour, she was spent. She excused herself for refreshments.

I took up a new position in the room, and I continued to use Male Body Language That Attracts Women. I directed my attention toward a decoration. Within five minutes, another woman who was far more attractive than the first came to me. She walked directly toward me and started my second conversation of the evening.

I enjoyed talking to her. During this encounter, I was amazed at the openness of how she revealed her personality to me during this conversation.

I used side-step standing positions and tightly-crossed knees sitting poses during our conversation. The encounter lasted for close to an hour.

I tried not to look directly at her, but gave her ample opportunities to look at me. I kept my arms behind my back as much as I could. I took several large breaths to expand my chest so she could see a profile of my pecks.

The reaction I received was astounding.

She said she wished she would bump into me more often. She told me she was not a good planner in life and liked to have events sweep her away. She leaned forward to me several times and touched my forearms. I remained relaxed and friendly the entire time. I made no overt or aggressive moves toward her.

She became more animated and more open as the conversation went on.

After a while, her husband appeared. He had been drinking in another room with his buddies.

He watched his wife for a few minutes, saw how animated she was, and moved directly between us. He kept his feet square and his shoulders square. He glared at her at one point because she seemed to be having such a good time talking to another man.

I remained totally non-aggressive during the entire episode. Because I was not as animated as his wife, I could not be interpreted as hitting on her. To him, it appeared I was standing there. She was the one who was excited.

Eventually, her husband caused her to move to another part of the party. You might say he herded her away like an English sheep dog by making it uncomfortable for her to be close to me.

Once his wife had moved into another room, he took up the conversation with me. I was polite. I knew his wife was becoming too friendly for her husband to allow it to go much further.

Why was this social event so successful for me?

Beside that I had used body language signals to attract these women, I gave up control of the conversations. I took the situations as they came. I stayed casual and relaxed.

Giving up control works especially well in business with women. I believe that most men try to control women through aggressiveness. It is refreshing for a woman to deal with a man who recognizes her authority.

Recently I was invited to attend a meeting in a large corporation by the woman who heads up the marketing group.

She took over her position about a year earlier, succeeding a man who had a strong personality. This woman also had a reputation for being tough. I found her to be a crackerjack manager who knows what she wants. I was invited to attend the meeting because she wanted to gather together everyone working on a major project. Her purpose was to focus all team players in a single direction and make the work go quickly and efficiently.

The instant we were introduced, she said to me, "I have always admired the work you have done for us. We have a big project now for you."

My response was, "Thank you. I will listen closely to make sure I give you what you want."

My male body language was casual, and I smiled pleasantly. I kept my arms behind my back during the conversation.

My feet were not square to her, but in the side-step position.

I looked her straight in the eye when I spoke to her, but I looked away appropriately not to appear aggressive or confrontational.

While she was a beautiful, finely attired woman, I never looked at her body.

She was immediately at ease with me.

I had told her verbally and non-verbally that she was in control and I would follow her wishes.

Throughout the morning meeting, I listened to her, asked questions that clarified direction, but did not challenge her with my body language, my eyes, or my words.

At lunch, I sat next to her in the corporate lunch room. When I finished eating, I sat with my legs tightly crossed, and angled them so she could easily view my genital area. I crossed my legs several times in the course of the fifteen minutes we talked. I listened mostly, and looked away as part of a thinking ritual.

I keep myself on display for her to enjoy, if she wished. I wanted her to be totally comfortable with me. I hoped I could stimulate her on some deep emotional level so she would want me to work on her project.

One month later when my work was submitted, it received an immediate, positive reaction. Some revisions were needed to my original work, and they went through smoothly. I remained responsive to her needs throughout the project.

Control is probably the most important emotional issue for you once Male Body Language That Attracts Women begins to work for you. Naturally, you want to be in control. Trying to be in control of the woman will stifle your efforts.

You must accept the fact that part of the success in building new relationships with women is that you must give up control. When you try to take control back, the entire structure of your fragile relationship can fold like a house of cards in a gentle wind.

I urge you to accept this view.

Male Body Language That Attracts Women works to cause women to come to you. Once this phenomena begins, you must play out the hand which is dealt and see where it leads.

If you are interested in attracting women, you must accept the fact that you have little control about *which* women you will attract. Make the most of each budding relationship, and more women will follow. You will learn from every encounter.

You will begin to know how to be more successful with the women you attract.

I believe your ultimate goal should be to establish friendships with women, albeit business friendships and loyalties in some cases.

These friendships can be powerful for you, and can lead to even more friendships that will benefit you in greater ways.

13.

Now it is your turn!

Since I have been using these body language techniques, I have had women who are complete strangers tell me things I would never have pried out of them if I was using my former aggressive, natural male body language.

Women take extra time with me, give me special attention in business, and go out of their way to praise my work.

You may want to use Male Body Language That Attracts Women to greater sexual and social advantage.

I encourage you to do so, particularly if you have been marginally successful in attracting women to you in the past. If you believe you are attractive, but for some as yet undiscovered reason, women have avoided you, it could be your body language is sending the wrong messages.

Try the techniques revealed to you in this book.

In the beginning, you will be learning how male body language works. You will use trial and error, as you feel your way.

You will learn new standing and sitting postures on your own. You may go overboard, and exaggerate a posture too much. If you do, try again and don't be so aggressive with how you display of your body next time. You will have many opportunities.

Remember, display is passive aggression.

Display of the male body is the lure that attracts women. You cannot predict what will come your way.

No matter what woman approaches you, stay relaxed and non aggressive. Let the woman lead and control the situation, and respond to her in polite, enjoyable and non-confrontational ways.

Other women are likely to be watching you the entire time. You may never notice them, but they are noticing you.

Based on your encounters and experiences, more women will eventually respond to your new found male body language skills. Use these techniques always.

I will leave you with this encounter:

I recently needed to be fingerprinted to apply for a special permit. A woman manager ran the fingerprinting department at the local police station. I was using Male Body Language That Attracts Women as soon as I entered the room because I observed the woman manager as well as another woman waiting to be fingerprinted. The second woman was young, smartly dressed and attractive. It might be nice to get her attention.

I didn't have a clue as to what might happen.

The woman manager lined all the applicants up. She placed me last.

A male sergeant came into the room.

The woman manager processed the paperwork for each applicant. Then, the male sergeant fingerprinted each of the applicants.

All the applicants were processed, except one: me.

Without my realizing it, the woman manager skillfully delayed processing my paperwork for a minute or two.

The burly sergeant became impatient. He had completed fingerprinting all of the applicants ahead of me. He was standing, waiting.

The woman manager turned to him at this point and said, "It's okay, Sarge. I'll finish up."

After he left the room, she completed my paperwork in a moment.

She took me to the fingerprinting station. With great care, she held each of my fingers, inked them and rolled them.

She handled me personally and gave me special attention. I didn't mind at all.

It wasn't a sexual encounter in any way. It was simply pleasant. It was much more gratifying to have this nice lady carefully handle me, than the burly sergeant.

I believe her extra attention resulted from my non-verbal communications that made this woman want to touch me and stand close to me.

Male Body Language That Attracts Women can work for you in many unexpected ways, just as it did for me this time.

I encourage you to think about everything in this book, avoid typical male aggressive postures and eye movements in the presence of women, and put your body on display in every subtle way you can think of, starting with the basic techniques described here.

The results will surprise and encourage you -- and enrich your life.

Acknowledgement

The clipart images in this book are the property of Corel Corporation and are used under license. No endorsement of this book and no association with the individuals in the images is expressed or implied. All clipart images were chosen by the author because they are expressive of his opinions which are his alone.

About the Author

Tony Wood has investigated, experimented and employed persuasive techniques for more than two decades. An award-winning advertising executive and former journalist, Tony Wood participated in body language experiments in college which led to his life long interest in the subject. Over the course of several years, he developed the body language techniques described in <u>Male Body Language That Attracts Women</u> through experimentation in both business and social settings. These techniques have been shared with other men and the astounding, eye-opening results are revealed in his book. <u>Male Body Language That Attracts Women</u> was written by Tony Wood to show more men how to excite and arouse women simply by the way they move near women, look at them, sit in their presence and stand near them. He is currently a marketing consultant for some of the world's largest corporations.